THE
SLOW
ROAD
COOKBOOK

**THIS BOOK
PLANTS FORESTS**

KIRIANNA POOLE

For my husband. Thank you for believing in me. It's hard to sum up my appreciation for you and your devotion to sharing my passion. Thank you for your love, patience and willingness to eat anything I put in front of you.

CONTENTS

HI, I'M...

Alba

Also known as Squishy. I love
unicorns and helping my mum
cook. I will eat absolutely anything
she puts in front of me, but golly
gosh, I love a doughnut.

Riley

I'm a free spirit and don't like
shoes too much. I love sharks
and the ocean. I could eat my
body weight in sushi.

Lockie

Also known as Dad, photographer, driver,
mechanic and packhorse. I'm always keen
for a good time around a fire and love
myself a few dozen oysters. I get excited
about pretty much everything and am
always on the lookout for a secret spot.

Izzie

I'm a VW Splitscreen Kombi, born in 1962. I love nothing more than keeping everyone safe and always try to break down as close to a town as I can.

Kiri

Also known as Mum, cook and DJ. I love yellow and never leave home without a hat! My love language is cooking for my family outdoors, and I've been on a mission to find the best bacon and egg roll in Australia.

Elsie

Also known as Little Bear. I love cuddles, broccoli and think my brother and sister are hilarious.

Bella

I'm a fibreglass Franklin caravan born in 1964. I got these guys off airbeds and onto comfy mattresses, so they all love me very much!

A JOURNEY WITH SLOW

It's because of Izzie that we embraced a slower life. She's our 1962 Kombi which Lockie and I bought in 2018 and fitted out for a lap of Australia. Riley, our son, was just 18 months old, but this journey taught us how little we needed to be content. Our days were all about early sunrises, soaking up family time, cooking with a different backdrop each day and watching sunsets. It was the adventure we'd been craving, and I didn't realise how happy it would make us.

Like all good things, it eventually ended. Lockie, a pilot, had to go back to work, so we found a suburban home and welcomed our second child, Alba, into the world. But then COVID hit, and it forced us to reassess. For us, it was a gift. It was an uncertain time, but we decided to move back into Izzie. We packed up our house and set off on our second lap of Australia. We never thought it would last two years, but who could have predicted anything that would happen during those times? We'd never lived more slowly or been happier.

Travelling slowly lends itself to a lifestyle of eating slowly. Australia is a wonderland for passionate cooks, where sustainable seafood, grass-fed beef and spring lamb are easy to get. There's plenty of space for foraging and heaps of roadside stalls with fresh fruit and veg scattered around the countryside. On long drives, I would spend hours dreaming up recipes, then bring them to life when we camped that night. Slow became an ideology of how I think about our food, summed up in the words seasonal, local, organic and whole (SLOW).

My grandparents set me on this slow food journey that started as a girl, growing up with them in New Zealand. They nourished a big garden full of vegetables, a wildly beautiful feijoa tree and even a space where my papa would dig holes in the lawn for a hangi (an earth oven). My grandmother had a knack for baking and slow stews, and her steam pudding fared well in the hangi. Our marae, the place our people come to gather, is where we learnt more about traditional food. In a Māori household like mine, there are many dishes that we love and share — my favourites are mostly seafood. We spent many weekends at my auntie's beach shack on the water, where my grandfather and uncle would go fishing and diving. As children, we would also head out, learning to thread our own lines and racing to catch the first fish.

I'd spend school holidays with Dad, a chef nicknamed Cookie. I was always watching and cooking with him. I remember teaching his apprentices how to cut onions and prepare meals the way he had taught me. Naturally, I waitressed for him when I was a teen, without knowing how valuable it was. Dad is a very patient man. He was calm and easy to learn from. Over my early teens, my excitement for food grew, thanks to Dad and his stress-free approach.

In my twenties, I savoured the fast-paced life of an air stewardess. I loved the excitement of different countries, food and people. I tasted my way around 60 countries, learning as much as possible before Lockie and I moved to Tokyo for six years in our late twenties. Japan is full of history and meticulous cooking. Century-old recipes are handed down through generations, their secrets closely guarded. Japanese cooks refine each dish to a level that amazes me.

I immersed myself as much as possible, but I yearned for a slower-paced lifestyle, which brought us back to Australia and influenced our Kombi adventures. We're now in New Zealand with a third child, Elsie (and a 1964 Franklin fibreglass caravan), in tow. This move has felt important, so our children can experience their Kiwi heritage, people, and ancestors. The transition to a slower-paced style of travel has also been perfect for our family. Together, and often at 80km/h (the speed our Kombi is happiest at), we have explored green lakes and homegrown gardens full of flourishing vegetables while we've connected with the land.

On the road, I've found that sharing meals is an excellent way to connect with others, maybe via lunch with friends, a celebratory dinner, or even when buying ingredients from local growers. It brings people together, it's why I love to cook and where I find my sense of mindfulness.

As a family, living slow is a priority, not only as the way we travel but also as a way of life. My own journey has been a humbling experience that I am grateful for. Now, I practise, share and encourage cooking with family and friends outdoors and together as often as possible. I have learnt so much in these past few years as a mumma, wanting nothing more than to now show as much of this beautiful world to my children as possible.

I'm sharing these recipes for the mummas like me, who crave a slower life, more connection with our families, the land and, just as importantly, ourselves. They aren't all of the journey, but they are some of it, and I hope they inspire you to slow down a little more in life and in travel.

Kirianna Poole.

CHAPTER 1

TIPS

Over the next few pages, you'll find all my tips, tricks and helpful information I have learnt from living on the road over the last five years. I also talk about what slow living means to me and how it has changed my life.

SLOW FOOD

CHOOSING SLOW INGREDIENTS

Travelling slowly means that we make frequent stops, like pulling over to buy prawns directly from trawlers or shopping at a farmers' market. I love these opportunities to get to know the local community. At farmers' markets, we can connect with people and have some great conversations, learn about seasonal foods and traditions, and help keep local growers employed. Buying food in a big supermarket cuts us off from this whole experience.

As we travel, we base our food choices on this mentality of slow. Summed up in four simple words, it reassures me I'm doing the best I can for my family, local communities and the people who grow and produce our food.

Seasonal: For maximum flavour, freshness, and nutrition, I recommend sourcing seasonal ingredients. If a particular food isn't in season, you can usually swap it for something that is.

Local: Buying locally grown, caught or hunted ingredients means supporting local people and reducing food miles, which is better for the planet. I love buying fruit and veggies from roadside honesty boxes and farmers' markets.

Organic: Choosing ingredients free from hormones and pesticides may cost more, but they're certainly better for your body. Organic foods often have more flavour, too.

Whole: We prioritise ingredients that are still in their natural state or that haven't been refined or processed. It's food straight from nature and food that makes our bodies feel awesome. The best places to find whole foods are at farmers' markets, roadside honesty boxes or foraging for them, which we love to do as a family.

SUSTAINABLE HABITS

With cooking comes scraps. Composting reduces our footprint into land waste. It might seem like a lot of work, but it is so beneficial and easy once you've formed a habit of doing it. The compost bin I've purchased is the sustainable Bokashi bin, and it's even made from recycled plastics. It ferments organic waste right here in my caravan with no odour or mould. The process is simple and so beneficial. Trying to do better and lessen my footprint is a long journey and one I'm really becoming passionate about.

REPURPOSING SCRAPS

Using every part of the protein when cooking is a great place to start. Things like broths, smoothies and dehydration can be a wonderful way to repurpose the scraps of certain foods. I try to organise my meals around best-before dates, logging them into my phone as a reminder.

USING THE WHOLE INGREDIENT

With storage in mind, I try limiting my scraps by using as much as possible in my food. Stems of herbs have amazing flavour — don't throw them away; grate them in. Egg shells can be crushed and added to soil. Boiling banana skins and utilising their natural nutrients of magnesium, potassium, and tryptophan can assist in sleeping and relaxing.

COMMUNITY GARDENS

I recently discovered community gardens, where they often have a composting area. I thought, "Why not carry a tub?" Last month, we stayed in a caravan park on New Zealand's South Island, where they had big scrap tubs in the kitchen. They also had a lovely happy herb garden out the front. I would love to see more of this in caravan parks. Fingers crossed.

PANTRY ESSENTIALS

PANTRY & FRIDGE

My grandmother's pantry is enormous; she stores enough for a few rainy days. Frankly, I think she is hoarding, but whenever I cook in her house, I know I'll always find what I need.

Prioritising what to store in a tiny home on wheels is difficult. After many years of cooking meals on the road, I have found a method to stay organised with my pantry and fridge. This method is very basic, so you can vary it to your needs. My Kombi's pantry has two small drawers and a 50-litre fridge. While towing a caravan now allows us to carry a few more things, for weight purposes, I still try to be as minimalistic as possible.

I try my best to buy seasonal, local, organic and whole ingredients whenever possible for maximum freshness and to support local growers while we travel. We are lucky to have a large variety of beautiful produce in Australia and New Zealand. I encourage you to substitute different ingredients as seasons change. To keep fruit and vegetables for later, I like to freeze mangos when they are in season, pickle vegetables, and cure lime skins.

FOOD FOR YOUR VAN'S PANTRY

These are the items that I keep in my van and caravan at all times:

Spices: Basic spices are all you need; you can mix them to enhance different meals.

My top eight spices and herbs are -

1. Paprika
2. Cumin
3. Cinnamon
4. Oregano
5. Dukkah
6. Chilli flakes
7. Black pepper
8. Flaky sea salt

Make sure they are in the same size jars so they stack together.

Storage containers: Separate your groceries into containers after shopping. Square containers are easier to stack.

Labels: There's nothing worse than rummaging for something in a small space. Try using a whiteboard marker.

Jars and cans: I try to make as much from scratch as possible, then store it in my fridge. I do, however, pretty much always have these items on hand:

1. Coconut cream - great for curries, fish and desserts
2. Tinned tomatoes - I like cherry
3. Homemade stocks - a range of vegetable and chicken
4. 00 flour and all-purpose flour - 00 flour is a must-have for pizza and pasta dough
5. Baking powder
6. Masa harina - for making tortillas
7. Tomato paste
8. Mustard powder
9. Wasabi powder – you can get tubes, but I like the powder
10. Chickpeas - a must-have for making hummus
11. Passata

Condiments

1. Kewpie – as big as you can get it
2. Fish sauce
3. Japanese soy sauce
4. Mirin
5. White miso paste
6. White wine vinegar
7. Red wine vinegar
8. Sesame oil
9. Extra virgin olive oil
10. Worcestershire sauce
11. BBQ sauce
12. Tomato sauce
13. Honey

COOKING WITH KIDS

Cooking is fun, and it helps ignite kids' creativity. Some of my most beautiful childhood memories are of cooking with my grandmother. I used to watch her every move, trying to replicate what she did. Whether she was making bread or cooking cakes, she had me in awe of the ease and simplicity with which she did it. These are the kind of memories that I am passionate about creating with my own children.

Here are some tips to get kids started in the fun world of cooking outdoors.

1. Get them to help collect and stack firewood. We usually construct log cabin fires (page 30), and kids have lots of fun with them because it's like playing a big game of Jenga.

2. Give them responsibility; it gives kids a great sense of purpose when they help cook. It's easy to hover over them constantly, but instead, give them a job and leave them to it. I find that simple tasks work well, like mixing ingredients or cutting soft foods with a butter knife.

3. Explain the dangers in each phase, especially when cooking over a flame. I will let the kids stir pots over the fire when I'm nearby, but I always explain the different parts of a fire and where the most heat is found. I constantly ask my oldest, Riley, about the three elements of fire (heat, fuel, and oxygen) and what happens if we take one of them away. Building this knowledge and foundation helps them understand fire and its dangers. In turn, they learn always to respect it.

4. Embrace the mess! Let them lick the spoon, get dough everywhere and eat as they go. Cooking with kids is messy, but that's also part of the fun.

5. Have them try new things and ignite their taste buds. Riley is not a fan of anything with too much flavour. But, when he cooks with me and sees how certain dishes are made, he is far more open to trying new things.

6. Get foraging! Whether you're walking along a river and picking blackberries or asking the kids to find the best tomato at a farmers' market, there is so much fun to be had. It teaches kids about where ingredients come from and the importance of looking after the land. We recently stopped at a growers' market where you could take a basket and pick the most amazing organic produce. For over an hour, we walked the fields, picking tomatoes and lettuce, and pulling beetroot.

GEAR

I cook outdoors a lot, and the following are staples that I can't live without. Cast iron is my favourite durable cookware. It holds heat really well and, if cared for correctly, can be passed down to your children's children. I recommend purchasing a storage bag so you don't get black charcoal marks everywhere!

Camp Oven: Not much has the same versatility, and if I could only have one item, a camp oven would be it. You can cook almost anything in them. Mine is 9qt, perfect for cooking for as few as two or as many as five or six.

Camp Oven Trivet: For certain meals in the camp oven, a trivet is handy to get the food off the bottom so it doesn't burn.

Skillet: I only carry one and use mine every day, whether I'm cooking on fire outside or with gas in the caravan.

Saucepan: A nice little cast iron saucepan is great for making sauces.

Billy Can: Useful for more than just boiling water over the fire, these are great for cooking pasta, too.

Tagine: Tagines are perfect for slow-cooked stews of meat, chicken, fish or vegetables. They date back centuries and have cone-shaped lids that allow steam to circulate and feed moisture back into the food below. Mine has a cast iron base that's great to use on coals. It also doubles as a serving dish.

Stock Pot: Essential if you plan on cooking crayfish and mud crabs. We carry a 12L version, but anything over 10L is fine. It's also great for stocks and broths.

Wok: Great for deep frying, quick noodles, rice dishes and reheating.

Campfire Grate: I cook with ours a lot, and next to the camp oven, it's our number two must-have. We've used many different ones but found our Oz Braai one the most useful as it can be flipped upside down and hung from a tripod to vary the height. I also have a smaller, simple grate. We use it for anything from cooking pipis down the beach to yakitori at camp. It was $20 and as light as a feather.

Campfire Tripod: Great for suspending your camp oven or billy.

Heat Resistant Gloves: Cast-iron cookware gets hot fast. Gloves are your best bet to avoid hot hands.

Camp Oven Lid Lifter: A great little tool to help lift a camp oven's lid while keeping the coals on top. We lost ours for a few months while driving around Australia, so we used the corner of an axe instead. It definitely wasn't as easy; a few lids were dropped in the fire!

Small Axe or Tomahawk: These are essential tools for cutting wood for your cook-ups and lifting lids off camp ovens when you lose your lid lifter.

Folding Shovel: Has an unlimited amount of uses. I use mine for hot coals, but they're also great for building sandcastles on the beach with the kids!

Knives: If I could only have two knives, it would be a chef's knife for daily cooking and a filleting knife for fish. Chef's knives are easy to handle, with a nice-sized blade for cutting meats and vegetables. Filleting knives are versatile and will save your thumb if you're filleting fish. Ours gets used a lot.

Mortar and Pestle: Before blenders, all sauces and rubs were made with this ancient essential. They have an endless life and come in various sizes (like lightweight travel ones) and materials like wood, bamboo, and even marble.

Good ol' Chopping Board: Mine is bamboo, lightweight and sustainable. I regularly sand it back and rub on a good food-safe mineral oil or wax to extend its life.

If your board ever begins to smell, run half a lemon across the surface; the acid will oxidise the bacteria and fats.

Meat Thermometer: A meat thermometer is a fantastic tool to take the guesswork out of cooking. Nothing is worse than overcooking and ruining a good piece of meat, and this will prevent that.

Fine Grater: You will notice a lot of grated ginger and garlic in my recipes. A grater is an easy addition to your utensils that can elevate your meals.

Picnic Rug: I never leave home without my Wandering Folk picnic rug – it has endless uses, from a beach rug to tablecloth to baby play mat. Lockie even lies on it when he fixes our Kombi!

BBQ or Pizza Oven: We used to carry a Weber Baby Q on the roof; it's a great little BBQ. We now just use a Gozney pizza oven. As well as pumping out amazing pizzas, it's great as an oven.

Portable Rotisserie: There are many well-priced, lightweight and portable battery-operated spits on the market that will change your camping game.

Utensils: Long tongs and wooden spoons work best for the fire. Other useful utensils include a ladle, a metal flipper, a rolling pin (alternatively, an olive oil or wine bottle works), a whisk and a serving fork to pull the meat.

COOKING WITH FIRE

A JOURNEY WITH FIRE

Cooking over an open fire is a glimpse into our ancestral past and so rewarding. It's a constant learning experience demanding patience, a watchful eye and comfort with the coals and temperature.

For our ancestors, fire was a vital part of life; it provided warmth, light and coals to cook over. I love the connection and primal instinct I feel when cooking over fire. Over the years, it has become my form of meditation.

When I was younger, I watched my Dad cooking this way. He taught me how to understand the coals, the wind and the flames, gradually building the heat and then moving the meat.

Travelling Australia by van, I didn't have much of a kitchen. I had a little outdoor gas burner, a fridge and a sink, but it was all I needed. That naturally led me to prepare and cook outside.

The simple elegance of a fire brings friends and families together. It's a place where you can unwind to share stories and memories. Listening to the crackling sound of wood while watching shapes that are forever changing creates a sense of calm.

In the following pages, I explain the basics of building a fire and how to cook on it. Fire cooking is not as precise as turning a dial to maintain heat; the fire will do whatever it wants, and we merely use some of its energy to cook. The conditions are ever-changing, as is the wood you use. These are my guidelines, and they may not be exact.

Learning to harness the fire takes time, but, in my opinion, no other form of cooking can replicate the flavours you can get from food cooked over open coals. By no means have I mastered it, and I am constantly humbled, but I have a deep respect and love for this ancient art form that will never tire.

In this book, I cook lots of recipes over fire, but they can all be cooked on a gas cooker or at home. The heats will all be very similar. I love cooking in a full kitchen when I have one! So put on the sound of a crackling fire, get cooking and start getting excited about your next adventure!

BUILDING
A FIRE

Building a good fire to cook on is all about preparation. I gather all the wood I think I'll need for the fire before lighting it. That way, I don't have to leave it once it's burning and risk losing control.

In Australia, bushfires are a real threat. Wherever we are, I always check the regulations to ensure lighting a fire is okay. If the wind's too high or it's really dry, we cook another way. No matter what, I always put my fire out at the end of the night and clean up the next morning, leaving the site as I found it. It's such a privilege to travel this beautiful world, and by respecting it and treating it right, we can leave the opportunity for our children to enjoy.

There are many methods to creating a good cooking fire, but, in my opinion, nothing gets you a good base of coals quicker than the 'log cabin'. Growing up in a Māori household, we often went to our marae for events where we'd sometimes feed hundreds of people. We would lay down a hangi, which is basically a massive earth oven, and the log cabin was our favourite way to build the fire. It's easy to make it big or small, depending on how many you are cooking for.

Start by collecting or cutting up some hardwood logs that'll burn hot and long. For an average fire, I'd use 25 to 35cm (10 to 14in) long timber and around 5 to 8cm (2 to 3in) wide. Obviously, for bigger fires, you can use bigger logs. I recommend about 12, though you may need more. Next, collect some kindling and tinder – I like dried grass or stringy bark.

Place small tinder in the centre of where you want the fire.

Lay down two logs parallel to each other, about a foot apart, on either side of the tinder. Place another two logs on top but perpendicular to the first two. Set your kindling along and perpendicular to the top two logs.

Repeat this process like a game of Jenga until you've reached the desired height, typically four to five layers.

Most of the time, you will need to light some dried grass (or other form of starter) on the outside and push it into the base of the fire with a stick.

The fire should burn naturally for around 45 minutes. As the fire breaks down, add more logs as required.

Once the fire has broken down to the point that embers appear, you're ready to harvest the coals and begin cooking.

FIRE CONTROL

There are four stages of a cooking fire: ignition, smoke, flame and embers. Embers is when we do most of the cooking. As the embers break down, the temperature becomes the most uniform, and it's when we'll find the most optimum heat to cook on.

I like to divide my fire into two parts. In one, I'm continuously adding wood to create coals; in the other, I lay a bed of coals farmed from the first.

Think of your grill as an element. Turn up the heat by lowering it or adding more coals. Raise it or remove coals to turn down the heat.

To gauge the fire's temperature, I go back to basics and use my hand. With my hand palm down, I slowly lower it to about 10cm (4in) above the cooking surface. How long I can hold my hand there will give me a reasonable indication of how hot it is.

Low	10 seconds
Medium–low	8–10 seconds
Medium	6–8 seconds
Medium–high	3–5 seconds
High	3 seconds or less

TEMPERATURES

A meat thermometer is a surefire way to pull the meat out at the perfect time. It's great to do it by feel, but if in doubt, it's better to check with a thermometer than to ruin the dish. I like to remove the meat 3 to 5 degrees before the target temperature, as it'll keep cooking as it rests for at least five minutes.

Cooking red meats, I take them from the heat at these temperatures.

Rare	45–50°C (113–122°F)
Medium-rare	55–60°C (131–140°F)
Medium	60–65°C (140–149°F)
Medium-well	66–69°C (150–157°F)

Cooking white meats and fish, I take them from the heat at these temperatures.

Pork	70–75°C (158–167°F)
Chicken	75–80°C (167–176°F)
Fish	63°C (145°F)
Salmon/Tuna	55–63°C (131–145°F)

CAMP OVENS

For Christmas one year, my sister gave me a Le Creuset. Bright red and solid, it was my first Dutch oven. I was obsessed. Playing with flavours and waiting to see how they fused after hours over heat was so exciting. It wasn't until we travelled around Australia that I started to shift those much-loved recipes to a cast iron camp oven, which became one of my favourite pieces of equipment. The sheer number of things you can do with it is mind-boggling. I use it as an oven, a deep saucepan, and by turning the lid upside down, it's a skillet. Sometimes I even use it as my outdoor microwave by wrapping food in foil and placing it on the lid to warm.

I use one a lot throughout this book. Even if you are at home or there are fire bans, a camp oven is an ideal pot on the stovetop or in the oven.

Here are a few things I've learnt from cooking with one:

• Don't place the camp oven directly in the fire. Lay a bed of coals far enough away that the heat from the fire will not interfere with your camp oven's cooking temperature.

• Think about the coal arrangement for the dish that you're cooking.

• When slow cooking, or for meals that require me to start at a higher temperature and then reduce the heat, I usually set the camp oven on a grate, as I can get to the coals easily. If you don't have a grate, you can place the camp oven directly on the coals on the ground, being mindful of the heat.

• If it's a dish you'd usually cook on a stovetop, like risotto, seafood chowder or mussels, only use coals below the camp oven or suspended on a grate. You won't need to add coals to the lid most of the time.

• If you'd typically cook a dish in an oven or slow cooker, such as a roast, stew or bread, spread the coals below and above, with a larger percentage on the lid. Placing too many coals directly under a camp oven will make it too hot and burn the food. Using a trivet to keep the food off the bottom of the oven is a handy tool for certain meals.

Here is a rough guide for coal placement, which you will learn to fine-tune as you go.

Baking	**80% top, 20% below**
Roasting or slow cooking	**70% top, 30% below**
Simmering	**20% top, 80% below**

I also listen to the sounds inside the pot and check it regularly to give me the best chance of having the meal turn out how I planned.

• Cast iron heats up quickly and holds that heat incredibly well. It's always best to start with a cool oven and add heat rather than starting too hot and having to reduce the heat.

• Rotating the camp oven every 20 to 30 minutes is good practice to ensure you don't get any hotspots. Turn the camp oven 90° one way and the lid 90° the other.

• Using soap or detergent in your camp oven can taint the flavour and require you to re-season it. After each cook, while the camp oven's still warm, wipe it clean using some paper towel (and hot water, if needed) until it's smooth inside. Once the camp oven is cool and thoroughly dry, lightly rub it inside and out with a high-smoke-point oil (like grapeseed or vegetable) and paper towel, then pack it away in its bag.

If your food starts tasting a little funky, or there are build-ups around the insides of the camp oven that you can't remove, then it's time for a re-season. You can do it on the fire, the BBQ or in an oven. There are plenty of in-depth videos about it online.

COOKING WITH A ROTISSERIE SPIT

There's something so enjoyable about cooking on a spit, especially when camping with family or friends.
You can feed lots of people, and the delicious scents will fill your campsite. We've always carried one with us on the road. Initially, we had one with two metal steaks that went into the ground and a battery pack that rotated it. Now, we carry a one-piece, battery-operated unit that can pretty much be suspended on anything and start spinning.

There are two methods I employ when using a spit. For the first, I cook meat over high heat for meals like gyros, picanha, and even a whole pineapple, cutting off cooked bits as we graze. The second, for meals like a beef spit roast, I cook much more slowly over more moderate heat until the meat is cooked to perfection.

Here's what I've learnt from cooking with one:

• Use quality charcoal. We often use binchotan, which is kiln-dried Japanese charcoal. I love its long burning, low flame and low smoke properties. Food tastes distinctly different cooked over it, and the flavour it gives meat and chicken puts it in a league of its own. There are many grades, which can get expensive, but you can pick up a box at your local Bunnings that will do a great job. I love that for any bits that don't completely burn, you can wait for them to cool and then re-light them again on your next cook.

The other charcoal I like to use is natural lump charcoal. Compared to regular charcoal, it burns cleaner, hotter and for longer.

• The height of the spit matters. The perfect height for grazing meals like gyros and picanha, where you're cutting bits off as they cook, is where you can only hold your hand above the coals for two to four seconds.

The perfect height for most meats you're roasting is where you can only hold the palm of your hand over the coals for five to eight seconds before having to move it. It'll ensure the meat cooks through and finishes with a nice crust.

• As the fat drips onto the coals, flare-ups are inevitable. The best way to deal with them is to watch where the fat drips each time the spit goes around and then push coals away with a shovel or tongs to make a gap in that area.

• Cooking times for different meats vary, and wind, air temperature and the size of your coal bed affect it. Here's a rough guide:

Beef	40 minutes per kg
Lamb	1 hour per kg
Pork	1 hour 20 minutes per kg
Whole Chicken	1.5 – 2 hours

CHAPTER 2

DAY STARTERS

I find so much pleasure in cooking breakfast. Getting off to a good start is important, especially if you have a long drive ahead or a full day of activities planned. There aren't too many rules to my morning starters – brekky, as we call it down here – can be quick, sweet, or savoury. Here you will find my family favourites and even discover what's close to my heart: leftovers repurposed into a wholesome breakfast.

CHORIZO TACOS

Eggs are such a simple pleasure. They adorn our plates most mornings. These fun, Mexican-inspired chorizo tacos are a memory from our honeymoon in Sayulita, Mexico. Served with a Bloody Mary, they are devilishly good and will kick-start your day.

2 uncured, spicy chorizo sausages

1 teaspoon of paprika

1 white onion, finely diced

$\frac{1}{2}$ a red capsicum, diced

250g of cherry tomatoes, diced

1 bird's eye chilli, deseeded and finely sliced plus extra for garnish

4 free-range eggs

1 large tomato, diced

extra virgin olive oil

juice of one lime (or lemon)

4 corn tortillas (page 232)

fresh coriander

an avocado

Bring a skillet to medium-high heat. Remove the sausage meat from the chorizo casing and crumble the meat in. *Chorizo is quite fatty, so there's no need to add oil to the skillet.* Sprinkle in the paprika and toss the sausage meat in the skillet for 3 minutes, or until golden brown.

Add half the diced onion, capsicum, cherry tomatoes, and chilli and cook until soft (about 3 to 4 minutes). Press each tomato with a spoon, squishing the juice to make a quick sauce.

Reduce the heat to medium and make 4 wells in the tomato and chorizo sauce. Crack an egg in each well and cook for 3 to 7 minutes, depending on your preference. *I like mine gooey, so I cook them for 3 to 4 minutes.*

While the eggs are cooking, toss the remainder of the diced onion with the diced tomato, a drizzle of extra virgin olive oil and a good squeeze of lime to make salsa.

Warm the tortillas straight over a flame or in a pan for roughly 20 to 30 seconds on each side. Then divide the eggs and sauce onto the heated tortillas.

Spoon the salsa over the top. Heavily sprinkle coriander and add fresh chilli and avocado to your liking.

Raw or uncured chorizo sausages are best. The skin is softer, making it much easier to remove. Find them at your local butcher or supermarket in the sausage section.

SALMON FRITTATA

To Lockie and me, Tasmania is a place that almost feels like it's back in time. We spent our time in little shacks hidden behind private bays where we foraged around with the kids. Our fondest memories are of mornings tucked away eating local salmon in this bubbling frittata.

½ cup of spinach

4 free-range eggs

¾ cup of milk

extra virgin olive oil

20g of unsalted butter

100g of sustainably caught smoked salmon fillet

½ cup of soft feta

chilli oil

Heat a skillet to medium heat and wilt the spinach with a dash of water. Remove it from the skillet and set it aside.

Whisk the eggs with milk until the mixture is fluffy. *I like to make it really frothy – when you eat the final mouthful, you will discover these airy egg pockets.* Add the spinach.

Heat the skillet to high and add olive oil and butter. *Now for the fun part.* Once your pan is nice and hot, tip in the egg mixture – it is best when it hits the hot pan and bubbles all over, then reduce the heat to medium.

Using a spatula, bring the sides of the egg to the middle. Do this once around the whole pan, then flake in the salmon chunks evenly and scatter the feta, allowing it to cook for about 8 minutes or until the eggs have cooked right through. *If you press on it, the eggs should have a buoyancy similar to a baked cake.*

Remove from the heat, drizzle chilli oil to taste and serve with crusty bread or my focaccia from page 226.

Frozen spinach or last night's sweet potato also works really well in this morning frittata. Heat them up before adding them to the egg mix. If you don't have chilli oil, chilli flakes are yummy too.

BLOM'S PORRIDGE

Lockie's Grandfather, Blom, made the world's creamiest porridge. His kitchen sat on the Nambucca River in New South Wales' mid-north coast, in a home of peace and love. Every night we were with him, he'd sneak off to soak the oats for the morning. The next morning, Blom always laid out his homemade poached fruits, yoghurt, All-Bran and milk next to the steamy porridge. He even had a dedicated porridge saucepan, and he used to oil it after every wash to stop the oats from sticking. Starting the day with a creamy bowl of oats and stewed fruit is magical, and I never expected, as an adult, how childlike and happy it could make me feel.

3 cups of your
  favourite milk

2 cups of whole oats

1 teaspoon of salt

POACHED PEARS AND PASSIONFRUIT

170g can of
  passionfruit pulp

juice of 1 lemon

2 cups of water

1 cup of sugar

1 cinnamon stick

a pinch of salt

2 whole pears, peeled
  and quartered

Place the passionfruit pulp, lemon juice, water, sugar, cinnamon and a pinch of salt in a saucepan and bring it to a boil. Stir until the sugar dissolves.

Add the pears to the saucepan and reduce the heat to a medium simmer. Cut a circle of baking paper to fit snuggly in the pot and place it on top of the pears to submerge the fruit in the liquid. *That will also help the pears keep their shape instead of stewing down.* Simmer for 15 to 20 minutes or until the pears are tender. Check them with a fork or skewer.

Once cooked, remove the pears from the saucepan with a slotted spoon leaving the liquid behind. Place them in a mason jar. Simmer the liquid with the lid off for around 15 minutes or until reduced to a nice thick syrup.

Pour syrup over the pears and allow it to cool before refrigerating. They will keep in the fridge for up to 2 weeks. *They are amazing on Weet-Bix or All-Bran as well.*

Stewed fruit done, gently heat one cup of milk in a non-stick saucepan until it begins to foam and bubble, then remove from the heat. Add the oats and salt, pop the lid on and then rest it overnight in the fridge. *That's the trick to making them extra creamy.*

In the morning, return your oats to a low heat, add another cup of milk, gently raise the temperature until it begins popping, and then lower the temperature back down. While slowly adding the last cup of milk, gently stir the porridge until glossy and creamy.

Serve in a bowl with pears and passionfruit on top, plus a sprinkle of All-Bran, if you like.

PULLED PORK BENNY

I am weak for a breakfast date and will bounce out of a warm bed for eggs, and easily eat them for dinner. I discovered this hearty breakfast using leftovers while we were in the Northern Territory. It's a simple hollandaise sauce drizzled over leftover pulled pork with yolky eggs. It's a little naughty and a lot of nice!

200g of leftover pulled pork

2 brioche buns

4 free-range eggs

HOLLANDAISE SAUCE

2 egg yolks

1 tablespoon of lemon juice

1 tablespoon of hot water

100g of butter, melted

salt and pepper, to taste

Start by reheating the pulled pork in a skillet with some leftover juice for 3 to 5 minutes, or until well heated through. Meanwhile, toast the brioche buns and set it all aside to keep warm.

Place a pot of water on the heat to simmer. Add the yolks, lemon juice, and water to a separate, heat-proof bowl. Pop it over the simmering pot of water and begin whisking while slowly pouring the butter into the mix. The sauce will start to thicken and expand. Once the hollandaise has thickened to a silky consistency (*if you draw a figure-of-eight in the back of a spoon and it stays put, the sauce is thick enough*), remove it from the heat and season with salt and pepper.

Poach the remaining 4 eggs. *I like to crack my eggs into a small teacup so there's no chance of shell going into the water. For the perfect poached eggs, add a cap of white vinegar to the simmering water and swirl it with a wooden spoon. Drop the eggs into the swirling water and cook to your liking.*

Assemble your benny by spooning the pork over the brioche buns, followed by the poached eggs and a generous lashing of hollandaise sauce.

When making hollandaise, go slow with the butter – too much too soon can cause it to curdle and go lumpy. And although you pour the butter slowly, whisk it quickly, or the yolks can scramble. If you don't have pulled pork, shaved ham or smoked salmon works great as an alternative.

SOURDOUGH FRENCH TOAST

Alba wakes up on Saturday mornings extra happy, usually bouncing about and singing her breakfast song, which is along the lines of, "It's morning time; let's have breakfast; the sun is shining". To be fair, you would be pretty happy, too, if you knew Saturdays are for French toast. So, before my coffee is brewed, her sweet tooth request begins with a whisk in hand. We love to make French toast together, especially with candied pecans and lashings of agave syrup.

4 large free-range
    eggs

¾ cup of milk

2 tablespoons of
    ground cinnamon

4 thick slices of
    sourdough

a knob of butter, for
    the pan

CANDIED PECANS

½ cup of whole pecans

4 tablespoons of
    agave or maple
    syrup, plus extra to
    serve

Be careful, candied pecans are addictive, but they're easy to make. Cut a piece of baking paper to fit the base of a pan and place it over medium heat. Add the pecans and syrup and let them heat and change to a honeycomb colour. It'll take around 4 minutes. Flip them over to coat the other side. Remove and set aside to harden.

Crack all 4 eggs into a bowl with milk and cinnamon and whisk until the mixture is bubbly and well combined.

Slice 4 thick pieces of sourdough and place them into the egg mixture, turning over to soak each side until the bread is soggy. *My mum often sprinkles some sugar on the bread at this point to create a crème brûlée effect as the bread fries.*

Heat a skillet over medium heat. Add butter and let it melt, turning a frothy, nutty brown. Place the eggy sourdough into the hot butter, cooking each side for 3 minutes or until golden.

Serve topped with agave or maple syrup and candied pecans.

As an alternative to making them in a pan, oven-roast your pecans with an assortment of nuts and seeds. Any kind of thick-cut bread works for this recipe — even raisin.

TOMATOES ON TOAST

My heart explodes in tomato season. As a child, I spent many autumn afternoons picking tiny cherry tomatoes from my grandmother's garden and popping them into my pockets. They are exceptional to snack on and delicious on bruschetta. More recently, I've been sharing this recipe, one of my favourites as a teenager, with Alba. It's so simple – hot, blistered tomatoes on toast with lotsa cottage cheese – but a little fancy, too.

---

a punnet of cherry tomatoes

extra virgin olive oil

2 garlic cloves

sprigs of thyme

4 slices of sourdough

100g of cottage cheese

salt and pepper, to taste

Generously coat the tomatoes in olive oil before placing them into a skillet with 1 of the whole garlic cloves and thyme over medium heat. After 5 minutes or so, they will begin to crinkle and blister. Cover with a lid and slowly simmer for another 2 minutes. Some tomatoes may break, but let them bubble away; you want them to be jammy. Once they are, remove them from the heat.

Brush thick sourdough slices with olive oil and place them onto a hot pan; flip to toast both sides. Remove when golden, and immediately rub a fresh, peeled garlic clove over the bread. *The garlic flavour is mesmerising and melts into the sourdough. Don't skip this step.*

Spread the sourdough with cottage cheese, and spoon the tomatoes and juices over the top.

Ricotta or burra cheeses are also lovely with tomatoes.

CROQUE MONSIEUR WITH CORNED BEEF

I took inspiration from French croque monsieur for this recipe. I tasted my first real croque monsieur in a little market outside of Nice while we were looking for croissants for Riley. I adore how this simple yet luxurious grilled sandwich can be even more interesting with leftover corned beef with this splendidly good cheese sauce. The flavours just marry so well together.

4 slices of sourdough

40g of unsalted
butter

1 clove of garlic

2 teaspoons of Dijon
mustard

200g of sliced corned
beef

2 slices of gruyere

**BÉCHAMEL
SAUCE**

20g of unsalted
butter

20g of plain flour

1 teaspoon of
mustard powder
or mustard

1 cup of milk

1 bay leaf — optional

100g of grated cheese

Get started on the béchamel sauce first. Melt the butter in a saucepan until it's frothy, then add the flour and mustard powder, mixing it continuously until it forms a ball.

Pour in the milk and begin whisking out the flour lumps.
Once smooth, add the bay leaf and gently fold in the grated cheese. Once the cheese has melted and the sauce is velvety, set it aside.

Brush the sourdough with butter and place it on a hot grate to toast each side of the bread. Run a fresh garlic clove over the sourdough.

Layer the sourdough with Dijon mustard, a healthy spread of béchamel, shaved corned beef, and a slice of gruyere. Top with the sourdough lid.

Place it back onto the hot pan for 2 minutes on each side and serve once it's nicely toasted.

QUICK AND EASY ON-THE-GO BREAKFAST IDEAS

Travelling can get hectic and busy, and sometimes we miss those healthy starts. So I try to pre-plan our meals for the long drive days. Though we aim to travel no more than three to four hours a day, we always try to leave early, so these quick and easy brekky starters can be fantastic to kick-start us on those big drive or adventure days.

CHIA CUPS

I began making chia cups in the Yarra Valley during jam-packed days of exploring, because most of our mornings started at 5am. At night, I would soak them in little jars to eat on the go in the morning – no mess and no fuss.

4 tablespoons of chia seeds

1 cup of coconut milk

2 teaspoons of agave syrup or honey

1 tablespoon of coconut yoghurt

1 ¼ cup of fresh berries

Mix the chia seeds, coconut milk and syrup in a small jar with a lid until all the seeds are covered.

Using a fork, smash 1 cup of the berries into the yoghurt and mix them into the chia, then keep it in the fridge overnight.

In the morning, top it with the remaining berries and eat it whenever you get the chance.

Make variations with pantry items like nuts and milk.
Date syrup is an excellent option, if you have it.
Frozen berries work a treat, too.

THE GRAZIER

Alba has a bento box that she loves to fill in each morning. Because of that, I pre-boil half
a dozen eggs and keep them in the fridge, mostly for her little morning graze, but also for an easy snack.

2 boiled eggs

2 slices of cheese

smoked salmon slices

4 slices of cucumber

half an avocado

$\frac{1}{2}$ a kiwifruit or apple slices

2 fresh medjool dates

peanut butter

2 sourdough slices

mashed banana

cinnamon powder

Quarter the boiled eggs and assemble your bento box with egg, cheese, smoked salmon, cucumber, avo and kiwifruit.

Deseed the dates and spoon peanut butter into the cavity.

Spread some peanut butter, mashed banana and a sprinkle of cinnamon on the sourdough.

APPLE BIRCHER

Bircher is my early starter go-to; an excellent way to start a summery morning.

1 cup of rolled or quick-cook oats

3 tablespoons of nut milk

3 tablespoons of natural Greek yoghurt

1 teaspoon of ground cinnamon

1 apple, grated with the skin on

½ tablespoon of diced Medjool dates

a squeeze of lemon juice

2 tablespoons of almond and apple slithers

Simply combine oats, nut milk, Greek yoghurt and cinnamon. Give them a good mix. Add the apple and dates, and stir them in with the lemon juice.

Place it into a jar in the fridge overnight, then in the morning, top with almond and apple slithers.

REAL FRUIT SMOOTHIES

MAKES: 1

PREP: 5 MIN

Smoothies are a great way to pack in all the good stuff. Riley, my very fussy son, enjoys this smoothie with baby spinach as a green Hulk mix, but, really, you can combine any of your favourite frozen berries, coconut, bananas and peanut butter.

½ cup of frozen, diced mango

1 frozen banana

1 cup of milk

¼ cup of coconut water

⅓ cup of whole oats

⅓ cup of natural Greek yoghurt

1 tablespoon of raw honey

Place the heavier frozen fruits in the bottom of a blender. Add milk, coconut water, oats, yoghurt and honey. Blitz until smooth.

CHAPTER 3

MEAT &
CHICKEN

Discover my spin on classic favourites I've made fun for outdoor living,
and join me in a deep love for traditional, cultural cooking over the fire.
I encourage you to source free-range or grass-fed proteins nurtured
the way nature intended. These options are far healthier for the animals,
the environment and, ultimately, you.

LOW & SLOW BEEF RAGU

I am deeply in love with Italian food and can sniff out a Bolognese from anywhere. I was in Bologna, Italy, while pregnant with Riley. I still feel it, "swollen hot feet and a football belly walking into a restaurant. "Ciao" comes from the kitchen, and I'm fed quickly. The Italians are family people, and when they saw a pregnant woman coming in, they were honestly serving before I could sit down.

What I adore about Italian cuisine is the connection between family and food. The joy of sitting together and sharing meals made with love — it's wholesome and contagious. I became obsessed with fresh, handmade pasta and devoted myself to recreating my memory of this special trip. I have been slowly cooking my own version over the campfire for a few years now with some small twists that may be naughty in the eyes of many Nona's. I'm regretfully sorry, but gosh, I can't bring myself to change it.

1kg of beef chuck, cut into thirds

extra virgin olive oil

cracked pepper

1 large white onion, diced

1 large carrot, diced

1 large celery stalk, diced

3 cloves of garlic, finely diced

150g of pancetta

1 teaspoon of oregano

$\frac{1}{2}$ cup of red wine

2 cups of beef broth

400g of passata

1 bay leaf

200g of cherry tomatoes

salt

500g of fresh pappardelle

3 cups of grated parmigiano reggiano

Prepare a bed of coals away from your main fire and place a grate above it so you can cook in a camp oven over medium-high heat – *hot enough that you can only hold your hand 10cm above the cooking surface for 3 to 5 seconds.* If you don't have a grate, put your camp oven straight on the coals, but be more mindful of temperature control.

Coat the beef with olive oil and season with cracked pepper. Sear the meat until each side is golden. Remove and set aside.

Reduce the heat to medium, add olive oil to the camp oven and sauté the onions, carrot, celery, garlic and pancetta for 5 minutes, or until onions are translucent. Sprinkle in dried oregano.

The wine is the veins of this dish. I recommend a bottle of merlot – half a cup for the ragu and the rest to enjoy while eating. Allow the wine to steam and reduce by half before adding the meat back in. Cover with the stock and passata, and add a bay leaf. Lid on.

Add about 70 per cent of your coals to the lid. Listen for a simmering sound and add coals as needed to maintain it. Let the ragu slowly cook for 2 to 2 $\frac{1}{2}$ hours, checking and stirring it every 30 minutes. *I like to rotate the camp oven one way and the lid the other on each check.* If it's too dry, add more stock, but you shouldn't need to. In the final hour, the sauce will thicken. Add the whole cherry tomatoes for the last 30 minutes.

Meanwhile, boil generously salted water in a billy or saucepan and cook the pappardelle until al dente. Fresh pasta only takes 3 to 4 minutes to cook.

Remove the ragu from the heat when the beef is so tender it's falling apart. Plate it with a mountain of parmigiano reggiano and serve with a nice glass of red you saved earlier.

Look for a piece of beef chuck with some nice marbling; it will melt in the pot. Sub the cherry tomatoes for canned; however, carrots, onion and celery are the holy trinity of this ragu. If there is leftover sauce, a pie is a perfectly delicious way to repurpose it. Add pastry to a jaffle or pie iron, fill it with ragu and generous amounts of parmesan.

ITALIAN MEATBALLS

One of the most delicious traditional foods to make its way from Italy to my table is polpette (meatballs). I was 15 when I started my classical studies class in high school and began learning Italian history. It sparked my fascination with the country and, even more so, its food. It's one of my favourite places in the whole world, and I've now travelled there over ten times, each time falling more in love than the last. Meatballs was the first recipe I researched and made, and it's still an absolute favourite today. This recipe is my take, and by no means completely traditional, but truly incredible around a campfire with my focaccia baked in a camp oven (page 226) or a nice fresh ciabatta.

THE MEATBALLS

1kg of ground lean beef (the highest quality you can find)

200g of pancetta, finely diced

1 cup of breadcrumbs

$\frac{1}{2}$ cup of milk

1 onion, finely diced

3 cloves of garlic, diced

$\frac{1}{2}$ a grated and strained zucchini

1 cup of fresh oregano

1 teaspoon of fennel seeds

1 tablespoon of smoky paprika

200g of parmigiano reggiano

$\frac{1}{2}$ cup of flat-leaf parsley

fresh basil

THE SAUCE

extra virgin olive oil

2 cloves of garlic, diced

1 shallot, diced (or small white onion)

$\frac{1}{2}$ cup of red wine

400g can of cherry tomatoes

1 tablespoon of balsamic vinegar

1 whole carrot, peeled and ends cut off

salt and pepper

Prepare a bed of coals away from your main fire and place a grate above it so you can cook over medium-high heat – *hot enough that you can only hold your hand 10cm above the cooking surface for 3 to 5 seconds.*

In a camp oven, sauté the garlic and shallot in olive oil for 3 to 4 minutes. Add half a cup of red wine and cook it off for 2 minutes.

Add the cherry tomatoes, using the back of a wooden spoon to break them down. Stir in balsamic vinegar and a whole carrot and let it simmer for 25 minutes while you make the meatballs. *The carrot is there to release its sugar content. It's an old Nona trick.* Season to taste, then set to the side of the grate to keep warm.

Combine the mince and pancetta in a mixing bowl. *I like fine pieces of pancetta, but bacon or pork mince works beautifully, too.*

In a separate bowl, soak your breadcrumbs in the milk. Squeeze the bread mixture until liquid is released (discard it) and you have a soft paste. Add it to the meat, followed by the very finely diced onions, garlic, zucchini, oregano, fennel, paprika, and half the grated parmigiano reggiano. *Dice the onion very finely or the meatballs can separate and fall apart.*

Squeeze the mixture together, binding the ingredients with your hands, then roll the meat into palm-sized balls. For best results, pop them into the fridge for 30 minutes.

Brown the meatballs directly on a grate or skillet at medium-high heat. Add them to the meatball sauce in the camp oven once they're golden brown and allow it to simmer for 30 minutes. Remove the carrot before serving.

Serve up with shavings of parmigiano reggiano, fresh parsley and basil alongside plenty of fresh focaccia or ciabatta. I highly recommend a drizzle of chilli oil or flakes.

Don't overwork the meatballs, which can toughen them up. If cooking at home, place the meatballs on a tray and bake them for 30 minutes at 180°C (350°F) before adding the sauce. These meatballs will keep in the fridge for 2 days and are perfect for shakshuka eggs. Add red capsicum, onion, garlic, and tinned tomatoes to a skillet with the leftover sauce. Once bubbling, crack in 4 eggs and cook to your liking.

SHARED SHREDDED BEEF

When Cuba opened back up for visitors, its old cars, rich history and the closest thing to a 1950s time warp had us packing our bags. No hotels had room, so we rented one from a local family. They adored Riley, who was just three months old and we fell in love with them and Havana. The smell of old cars fills the bright streets, and musicians play on every street corner. This recipe takes inspiration from the mouth-watering dish ropa vieja. It brings everyone together and is best served straight from the camp oven with a stack of corn chips and good crew!

1.2kg of beef chuck

salt and pepper

extra virgin olive oil

100g of fresh, spicy chorizo, de-skinned

1 white onion, diced

3 cloves of garlic, finely diced

1 red capsicum, diced

1 cup of beef bone broth

400g tin of red kidney beans

1 cup of passata

200g tin of chipotle in adobo sauce

$\frac{1}{3}$ cup of pineapple juice

1 avocado, sliced

1 red chilli, sliced

the juice of 1 lime

a bunch of coriander

corn chips

Prepare a bed of coals away from your main fire and place a grate above it so you can cook in a camp oven over medium-high heat – *hot enough that you can only hold your hand 10cm above the cooking surface for 3 to 5 seconds.* If you don't have a grate, put your camp oven straight on the coals, but be more mindful of temperature control.

Pat the beef dry with a paper towel, and trim the excess fat — some fat is okay. Cut it into 3 chunks, season well with salt and pepper and coat it with a rub of olive oil.

Brown the pieces of beef until caramelised - about 2 to 3 minutes on each side. Remove them to a plate.

Add the chorizo to the camp oven and crumb it with the back of a fork to break it into pieces.

Remove some coals to reduce the heat to medium and sauté the onions, garlic and diced capsicum for about 5 minutes until lightly brown. Pour in the bone broth and return the beef to the camp oven with any juices left on the plate. Add in the kidney beans, passata. Mash or puree the chipotle and add it in with the pineapple juice.

Add 70 per cent of the coals to the lid. *Listen closely for a simmering sound and add coals as required to maintain it.*

Let the beef slowly cook for 2 to 2 $\frac{1}{2}$ hours. Check every 30 minutes and stir. *I like to rotate the camp oven one way and the lid the other on each check. If it needs more bone broth, add some if the meat has been on less than 2 hours.* It's done when you can twist a fork in it and it breaks apart, ready to shred.

Serve it straight from the camp oven with avocado, fresh chilli, lime juice, coriander and corn chips.

BEEF BRISKET PLATE

I have been weaving my way through flavours for well over a year now, eager to discover my own take on this loved American classic. When we lived in a house, we always had a smoker. It was one of the things I have missed living on the road. But recently, Traeger has released a small, portable pellet grill originally designed for tailgating in the USA. It takes a while (75 mins per 0.45kg), but having a few IPA's with your mates around camp for the day with the beautiful scent of slowly smoking brisket isn't too bad! Any leftovers are awesome on pizza.

1.5kg - 2.5kg brisket

1 ½ tablespoons of diced chipotle

2 tablespoons of paprika

1 tablespoon of dried oregano

1 tablespoon of cumin

1 teaspoon of ground coriander

1 teaspoon of chilli powder

2 tablespoon of garlic granules

1 teaspoon of onion powder

1 teaspoon of salt and pepper

1 cup of apple cider vinegar

2 cups of beer

1 tablespoon of Worcestershire

Prepare your brisket by trimming any excess and hard fat with a sharp knife to a thickness of 6-7mm (¼in).

In a medium mixing bowl, add chipotle, paprika, oregano, cumin, coriander, chilli powder, garlic granules, onion powder, salt, and pepper for the spice rub.

Rub it into the brisket generously and leave it to rest for 3 to 4 hours or overnight in the fridge. Before beginning the cook, bring the meat to room temperature (which takes about an hour).

Preheat your smoker to 110°C (230°F). We use Traeger Signature Blend pellets but hickory or mesquite are also lovely.

Place the brisket with the fat side towards the heat source (each smoker is different) and insert a probe thermometer into the thickest part of the meat to monitor the internal temperature. Shut the hood.

Mix the vinegar, beer and Worcestershire in a spray bottle to make a mop sauce and spritz the brisket with it every 30 to 45 minutes until you encounter a stall in its rising temperature – which will normally occur between 65 to 75°C (149 to 167°F). How long it takes to get to this point will depend largely on the size of the brisket.

I pull the meat off at 70°C (158°F), wrap it in butcher paper, then reinsert the probe and shut the hood.

Continue smoking until your probe reads 96°C (205°F), adding pellets as required. Remove the brisket from the grill and let it rest, covered, for 30 minutes.

Arrange on a board with slaw, mac cheese (both page 206), plum sauce (page 212) and, cornbread (page 231). Crack a beer and enjoy!

PICANHA

When it comes to steak, there are many ways to cook it. One of my family's favourites is spinning a picanha on a rotisserie. Picanha is a Brazilian style we know in Australia as a rump cap. It's widely available; just ask your local butcher. This mouth-watering cut of beef has a thick layer of fat, and by spinning it over charcoal at high heat, the fat will render down and flavour the meat. We first discovered this at a Brazillian BBQ restaurant in Malta, but the traditional way to enjoy it is to cut pieces off as it cooks. We are hooked. You're about to be, too!

chimichurri
  (page 218)

1.5kg of beef rump
  cap

4 tablespoons of salt

2 tablespoons of
  freshly cracked
  pepper

This pairs great with either sweet potato salad (page 196) or broccoli salad (page 192). Have rotisserie pineapple (page 252) for a traditional dessert. Put it on when the last of the picanha is off the spit. I first discovered gravy rolls in Australia, and the leftover steak is perfect in fresh rolls with thick butter and a rich gravy.

Get a campfire going so there's a nice bed of coals, or if you use charcoal chimneys, 2 loads are perfect.

Prepare a batch of chimichurri. *It needs 30-40 minutes in the fridge, so start it while the fire's settling in.*

Use a sharp knife to remove the stringy fat from the underbelly of the meat. I also trim back some of the top layer of fat to even it out. I want most of the fat to render and flavour the meat, so I leave at least 2cm (4/5in) of fat.

With a sharp knife, cut the rump cap across the grain into slabs approximately 3 fingers thick. With 1.5kg of meat, you should end up with 3 large pieces and 1 small tail. (*The tail is too small for the skewer, but it's a nice piece of steak so I normally sear it off and give it to the baby...*)

Next, thread the 3 large pieces onto the spit shaft in C-shapes, so the shaft passes through the top and bottom of the C, fat side out. I lay the pieces out and curve them to make Cs, then make an incision in the fat with my knife before threading them onto the rotisserie shaft. Firmly push the pieces together and secure them with the spit prongs.

Season both sides of the meat generously with salt and pepper and set the spit over the coals at a temperature where you can only hold your hand palm-down for 2 to 4 seconds.

Traditionally, once the outside layer is cooked (around 20 minutes), meat is sliced off, served, and the spit is re-salted and put back on to cook the next layer. That's what we do.

If you want to cook the meat entirely in one go, let the rotisserie spin until the internal temperature reaches 55 to 60°C (131 to 140°F).

Serve with my chimichurri.

WASABI STEAK

10 years ago, if you had told me to try some steak with wasabi, I would have looked at you like you had two heads. But, after living in Japan, steak and wasabi are two things I regularly combine.

While travelling Australia, Lockie and I would get a nice piece of high-grade wagyu to share on special occasions. A lot of people might think it's too expensive, but with good wagyu, you don't need much, and even the smallest mouthful is bursting with flavour. As wagyu is so rich, the tang of wasabi is a match made in heaven.

150 - 200g wagyu,
  marble score 5+

salt and pepper

30g of fresh wasabi

salt, to serve

Allow the wagyu to come to room temperature for around 20 to 30 minutes.

Heat a skillet to high heat. *If you have an infrared thermometer, you are looking for a pan temperature of 220°C.* If cooking over a fire, I highly recommend using a skillet instead of the grill, as the fat content causes lots of flare-ups, and you don't want to share this incredible fat with the fire, but rather, let the steak render in its own juices.

Season the steak lightly with salt and pepper, and trim a small piece of wagyu fat to grease your pan. Or use butter.

Sear the steak for 2 to 3 minutes per side. For a rarer steak, aim closer to 2 minutes. For a medium steak, aim closer to 3. *The higher the grade, the rarer you can have it.* Allow it to rest for 5 minutes.

Prepare a tasting board with a pile of wasabi and a pile of salt, and slice the steak into 3cm (1in) thick strips. Dip the steak in wasabi, then salt and go to food heaven with each bite. This pairs excellently with my Japanese cabbage salad on page 201.

I recommend a wagyu with a marble score of 5 or higher. The higher the marble score, the smaller the steak you will require. Cook highly marbled wagyu hot and fast. Wagyu should require little to no seasoning – the steak is the star here, so let it shine.

STEAK SANGA

Lockie has a love affair with steak sandwiches. It goes back to living in the hinterland of New South Wales, surrounded by cattle on his parents' farm. Travelling around Australia, he couldn't bear to pass a roadhouse or small town without trying the local version. He believes that is where the best of them is found. After many stops, I've learnt what makes a great sanga. I created this one for him.

a batch of mushroom sauce (page 213)

1 tablespoon of olive oil

salt and pepper

250g of grass-fed sirloin steak, brought to room temperature

4 slices of sourdough or my focaccia (page 226)

butter, to spread

1 clove of garlic, peeled

Jarlsberg slices

Prepare a bed of coals away from your main fire and place a grate above it so you can cook in a skillet over medium heat – *hot enough that you can only hold your hand 10cm above the cooking surface for 6 to 8 seconds.* Prepare a batch of mushroom sauce.

That done, add more coals to bring the heat up to medium-high (*a 3 to 5 second hand hold*). Meanwhile, oil and season the steak with salt and pepper.

Place the steaks straight onto the grate and press them down firmly to begin the seal and crust, then cook to your liking. Keep a close eye on the coals, and don't let the temperature drop – the occasional fat drip will help this. I like to flip and seal the other side after 2 to 3 minutes; I do this twice and crisscross the steak, purely to remind myself of my cooking time.

When the steak is done, remove it from the heat and set it aside to rest before slicing it into 2cm strips.

Butter 2 pieces of chunky sourdough or my focaccia and grill it over the grate for 2 to 3 minutes until lightly toasted. Rub the warm bread with a clove of garlic until it melts away, then layer the Jarlsberg, steak and a mountain of mushroom sauce.

Devour.

BLACK PEPPER BURGER

A burger is my feel-good treat – there is something special about beef, bacon and cheese. We love camping at outback stations, but our favourite is Bullara in Western Australia. It had such great energy, with animals for the kids, live music, incredible scones, and a burger night every Friday. The owners suspend a big hotplate above a fire and cook hundreds of burgers. My burger is an ode to the good people we meet and the experiences we have while travelling. After all, that's why we do it, right?

500g of quality, grass-fed ground beef

½ tablespoon of American mustard

½ tablespoon of salt

1 tablespoon of freshly ground black pepper

100g of streaky bacon

4 slices of Swiss cheese

4 fresh burger buns

butter, to spread

tomato sauce, optional

200g of rocket or iceburg lettuce

2 large truss tomatoes, sliced

1 red onion, sliced into rings

1 tablespoon of burger pickles

SPECIAL SAUCE

4 tablespoons of Kewpie mayonnaise

1 tablespoon of American mustard

2 diced dill gherkins

1 tablespoon of gherkin juice

½ teaspoon of paprika

1 tablespoon of diced white onion

After a bit of a change? You can substitute ground beef for ground turkey or swap the cheese for something robust, like a blue. For extra-crispy bacon, start cooking it in a cold pan without preheating, which renders the fat slowly.

Prepare a bed of coals away from your main fire and place a grate above it so you can cook over medium-high heat – *hot enough that you can only hold your hand 10cm above the cooking surface for 3 to 5 seconds.*

Mix all the special sauce ingredients and put it in the fridge while the flavours meld.

Combine the beef, mustard, salt and pepper in a bowl. Squeeze the meat to combine, then divide the meat into 4 even balls. Toss each patty from hand to hand to bind; the harder, the better for a good bind, so you don't need to use egg or breadcrumbs.

Place the burgers on the grate and press them flat. Cook for 4 to 5 minutes before flipping. At the same time, cook the bacon until it's crispy.

Just as the patties are finishing, place a slice of cheese on each one so that it melts. Add the cut buns, to the grate and lightly toast, then butter.

Spread the special burger sauce on the top bun using the back of a spoon and I love a healthy squeeze of tomato sauce on the bottom bun. Top it with lettuce, patty, tomato, onions, bacon, and burger pickles. *They are a must-have!*

Wash it down with an icy cold IPA.

CHIMICHURRI VENISON

Wild venison is a highly sustainable meat. It's a great source of protein and compared to other meats like beef, its levels of saturated fat are far lower. Venison is a very popular meat in New Zealand, and my family enjoys it regularly. If you haven't tried it, I highly recommend it, especially accompanied with chimichurri.

chimichurri
   (page 218)

500g of venison
   backstrap, at room
   temperature

1 tablespoon of extra
   virgin olive oil

1 clove of garlic,
   crushed

salt and pepper, to
   taste

Prepare a bed of coals away from your main fire and place a grate above it so you can cook over medium-high heat – *hot enough that you can only hold your hand 10cm above the cooking surface for 3 to 5 seconds.*

Prepare a batch of chimichurri. *It needs 30-40 minutes in the fridge, so start it while the fire's settling in.*

Meanwhile, mix olive oil, garlic, salt, and pepper in a bowl. Place the venison in the marinade and let it sit while the grill or skillet is heating.

Grill the venison directly on a grate (or in a skillet) for 3 to 4 minutes each side.

Remove the venison from the grill to a plate and rest it for 10 minutes before slicing and serving with chimichurri.

Sweet potato mash is the perfect match for this meal. There's a great recipe for it as part of the camp lamb shanks on the next page.

CAMP LAMB SHANKS

SERVES: 2-4

COOK: 3 HOURS

PREP: 10 MIN

Slow-cooking meat with its bones is a great way to fuel your body with rich nutrients. The bones gradually release collagen, glutamine, vitamins, and healthy fats as they cook, supporting a healthier gut. This cooking method has been practised for generations across many cultures and is still my favourite form of cooking. I was lucky enough to stay on a cattle and sheep farm along the Coral Coast of W.A. The farmer had a freezer full of his organic lamb. Of course, we took the opportunity to grab a few shanks and light up the fire.

4 lamb shanks

$\frac{1}{2}$ cup of flour

1 tablespoon of hot mustard

1 onion, diced

2 carrots, diced

4 cloves of garlic

2 sprigs of rosemary, roughly chopped

1 tablespoon of smoked paprika

50g knob of butter

$\frac{1}{2}$ cup of red wine

2 $\frac{1}{2}$ cups of organic beef broth

1 bay leaf

2 cups of passata

2 big sweet potatoes

extra virgin olive oil

$\frac{1}{3}$ cup of milk

1 cup of sour cream

salt and pepper

Prepare a bed of coals away from your main fire and set a camp oven on it so you can cook over medium-high heat – *hot enough that you can only hold your hand 10cm above the cooking surface for 3 to 5 seconds.*

Dust the lamb shanks with flour and coat them in mustard. Sear them straight on your grate until each side is golden.

Add the onion, carrots, garlic, rosemary, paprika and half the butter to a camp oven. Move them around until the carrots soften, the onion is translucent, and the paprika is fragrant. Add in the shanks.

Deglaze the camp oven with red wine and reduce until a third is left. After about 5 minutes, it will become lovely and glossy. Be sure to stay close to avoid burning.

Add half a cup of stock with a bay leaf and stir in the passata. This is the glorious start to the gravy. *It doesn't need to cover the shanks completely, but move them around each time you check them.* Place the lid on and add 70 per cent of the coals to it. *Listen closely for a simmering sound and add coals as required to maintain it.* Cook it for 2 to 2 $\frac{1}{2}$ hours, checking every 30 to 45 minutes, adding stock bit by bit, and giving it a stir each time.

Pierce the sweet potatoes with a fork all over, drizzle them with oil, and wrap them in foil with a the rest of the butter. Place them directly in coals away from flames for 30 minutes. Take them out of the coals and mash them with a fork, adding milk, salt and pepper.

Remove the shanks from the sauce and cover to keep warm. Add sour cream to the pot to make a creamy gravy.

Serve the shanks on the potato and ladle over some gravy. Garnish with slithers of lemon rind.

With leftovers, mash the meat and potato together. Heat a pan with oil and spread in the mash. Serve with an egg on top.

PISTACHIO LAMB KOFTAS

I'm sure everyone has a camping memory that stands out above the rest. After we last crossed the Nullarbor, we headed to the Eyre Peninsula to meet some of our good friends who also travel in Kombis. We spent three magical days swimming, chatting and having big cook-ups on the fire at night. Camping, for me, is about connection, whether with people, the ocean, or the land. It's the part I love the most and the part that keeps me coming back for more. These koftas are one of the meals I cooked for the crew during those blissful days.

4 - 6 flatbreads
  (page 230)

tzatziki (page 215)

1 shallot, finely diced

2 garlic cloves, grated

a handful of mint

90g of unsalted
  pistachios, diced

juice and zest of
  1 lemon

1 teaspoon of cumin

1 teaspoon of sumac

500g of organic
  ground lamb

6 metal skewers

extra virgin olive oil

2 truss tomatoes

1 Lebanese cucumber

½ a red onion

salt and cracked
  pepper

1 lemon, quartered

Prepare a bed of coals away from your main fire and place a grate above it so you can cook over medium-high heat – *hot enough that you can only hold your hand 10cm above the cooking surface for 3 to 5 seconds.*

Meanwhile, prepare some flatbread dough and make a batch of tzatziki. Set them both aside.

Combine the shallot, garlic, mint, pistachios, lemon zest, cumin and sumac in a bowl with the lamb mince. Roll the meat mixture into 6 even balls, tossing them between your hands to bind the meat.

Roll the meatballs into log shapes. Thread them onto metal skewers, and squeeze the meat tightly to secure it.

Brush the meat with olive oil before placing it on the grate to cook for approximately 8 to 10 minutes, turning regularly.

Meanwhile, quarter the tomatoes, dice the cucumber, and slice the red onion. Combine them in a bowl, toss in olive oil, and then season with salt and cracked pepper.

Place the flatbread on the grate and cook for 2 minutes a side.

Remove koftas from the heat, place in flatbread and slide meat off the skewer, smear on some tzatziki, add salad mix and a squeeze of lemon juice.

HANGI

As Māori, we have a strong connection with our whenua (land), which we are considered the kaitiaki (guardians) of. We acknowledge our ancestors and protect and sustainably nourish the land to pass on to our future generations.

I am from the iwi of Ngati Porou, Te Whānau-ā-Apanui, and Ngā Puhi, a region on the east coast of the North Island of New Zealand. It is where the ocean meets the mountains. My grandfather grew up on his family farm full of sheep that freely grazed the mountainous land, foraging through manuka trees and other natives.

My marae of Potaka is where I enjoyed many hangi (an earth oven), our traditional form of cooking. A hangi isn't just for large groups or celebrations. This form of slow earth cooking can be enjoyed as a family anytime, and though it takes some work, it is well worth the heat.

My children have been travelling their entire lives, so it is up to me to ensure they experience this special tradition from home. So, we have been practising it as a family of five often. Following is Papa's method, which he explained to Mum and me. While we chatted, he reminisced about our Christmases and how digging a big hole in the backyard brings our family together from all over.

I have altered the method only slightly, as some items we use in New Zealand (metal baskets and volcanic rocks) are typically harder to find elsewhere. As described below, you can make one with everyday items.

One of the beauties of a hangi is the sheer amount of people it can feed. I have seen many hangi feed 300 or more people. I really hope you give this a go and enjoy it. The taste of the earth that a hangi provides is unique and beautiful.

extra virgin olive oil

1 teaspoon of finely
chopped fresh
rosemary

savoy cabbage leaves

2 - 3kg leg of lamb

4 purple kumaras

4 potatoes

4 sweet potatoes

1 pumpkin

bunches of rosemary

steamed greens

fry bread (page 228)

MUMMA'S STUFFING

A day-old loaf of
bread, crumbled

200g of unsalted
butter

1 onion, finely diced

2 - 3 tablespoons of
dried mixed herbs,
to taste

1 whisked egg,
optional

$\frac{1}{4}$ teaspoon of salt and
pepper

HANGI ESSENTIALS

12 - 15 river rocks or
volcanic stones

hessian cloth - find
them it in hardware
stores or fruit shops

cheesecloth -
available from most
supermarkets

a new cotton sheet

a spade

2 enamel roasting
dishes

aluminium foil

Collect 12 to 15 very dry river rocks that are
at least bigger than a fist. *They will be the heat
source for the hangi. At home, we use volcanic stones,
but river rocks are a good substitute in Australia. Use
caution to avoid ones that are waterlogged or have
cracks in them, as they will explode. Find nice smooth-
edged rocks from the higher parts of a riverbed.*

Soak the hessian, cheesecloth and cotton
sheets in water. *Overnight is ideal, but for a
few hours while the fire burns down is no problem.
Wring them out before using them.*

Dig your hangi hole. *Make sure the location is
in a clean and safe area. Mark out your hole by
making cuts in the ground using the spade. It is best
to make a rectangle shape. For 4 to 6 people, a hole
80 by 45cm and 60cm deep will be perfect
(30 by 18 by 24in).*

Build a large log cabin fire (page 30) right
near the hole (*because we get the rocks from the fire
to the hole with shovels when they are hot*), placing
rocks on each level and top as you go. Set it
alight and allow it to blaze for 3 to 4 hours,
ensuring the rocks are white hot. Meanwhile,
begin preparing the food.

Mix olive oil and chopped rosemary in a bowl.
Line an enamel roasting dish with 2 layers
of cabbage leaves and put the lamb on top.
Brush the lamb with olive oil and rosemary
coating it well, season with salt and pepper,
then place 2 layers of cabbage leaves on top.
Wrap the entire dish in foil.

Dice all the potatoes and pumpkin leaving the
skins on, and simply coat them in olive oil and
place them into another roasting dish with
2 layers of cabbage leaves below and on top.
Wrap the entire dish in foil.

For Mumma's stuffing, grate the bread into
crumbs. Melt the butter into the onions
and pour it over the bread. Mix in the herbs
(*and add a whisked egg if your mixture is too dry*).
Season with salt and pepper.

Roll the stuffing into a log and wrap it in a damp cheesecloth. Wrap that in 2 layers of cabbage leaves and then in foil.

Now we pack and cover the hole. Once the fire has burnt down and the rocks are white hot, use a long-handled shovel to extract them and place them gently in the bottom of the hole. *We hit the rocks with the wet sacks a few times – the water helps create steam.*

Throw the bunches of rosemary onto the rocks and place the meat tray on the rocks, with the vegetables and stuffing on top.

Cover it all with the wet cotton sheet, followed by the 2 layers of wet hessian. *Lay them down slightly offset from each other so that you can pull the hessian away when you uncover it without letting dirt fall into the middle of the hole.* Gently fill the hole with dirt ensuring no steam is escaping. Note the time. It's best to leave the hangi to steam away for 3 to 5 hours, depending on the size and amount of meat.

Papa says there is an art to uncovering a hangi. Scrape with a shovel from the middle to the edges until you find the sacking. Be careful as it will still be very hot. Peel the first sack from the middle outwards, ensuring all the dirt falls away from the centre. Continue until you reach the dishes. Use oven mitts to pick them up.

Unwrap the meat and veggies and carve the meat. Serve with steamed greens and my fry bread.

A hangi is to be shared, and we always begin by blessing our kai (food). When we give thanks for the kai, it is known as a karakia. This is the one I grew up with -

E te Atua
Whakapainga ēnei kai
Hei oranga mō ō mātou tinana
Whāngaia hoki ō mātou wairua
ki te taro o te ora
Ko Ihu Karaiti tō mātou Ariki
Ake, ake, ake
Amine.

If you have a large group or family gathering, it's best to track down some metal hangi baskets. Then you can pop in as much meat and veg as you like and simply layer them in the same order described above. Just make the hole bigger and collect more rocks. Also, garlic can overpower the hangi, so it is best to avoid using any.

GOZLEME

My sweet memory of these perfect little parcels came from a week in
Cappadocia, Turkey. We spent Riley's first birthday eating breakfast on a balcony
taking in the magical view of dancing hot air balloons that floated past.
I remember this day so clearly because it is when he took his first steps.
We spent our time wandering paved roads to the main town, where aromas
of spices filled the streets, and we discovered traditional clay pots filled with
slow stews and little stalls serving gozleme. I quickly became addicted and
now love to make my own.

2 cups of natural
  Greek yoghurt

250g of self-raising
  flour

1 tablespoon of salt

1 teaspoon of smoky
  paprika

1 lemon, quartered

SPINACH AND FETA FILLING

200g of spinach,
  chopped into
  lengths

100g of feta

1 free-range egg

juice of 1 lemon

LAMB FILLING

extra virgin olive oil

1 shallot

2 cloves of garlic

1 teaspoon of cumin

1 teaspoon of ground
  coriander

200g of lamb mince

In a mixing bowl, add the yoghurt, then sift in the flour, salt and paprika. Use your hands to mix it and begin forming a ball.

Dust a workspace with flour to knead the dough into a shiny ball. *The dough will remain sticky.* Divide it into 4 even pieces, cover, and let them rest for at least 30 minutes.

Meanwhile, prepare a bed of coals away from your main fire and place a grate above it so you can cook over medium-high heat – *hot enough that you can only hold your hand 10cm above the cooking surface for 3 to 5 seconds.* If your grate has a hot plate, use it; otherwise, heat up your biggest skillet.

For the spinach filling, wilt the spinach in a pan, adding lemon juice as it cooks. Remove from the heat to a bowl to cool. Once it has, add the crumbled feta, egg, salt and pepper and mix well.

Meanwhile, sauté the shallots, garlic and spices in olive oil for 4 to 5 minutes. Add in the lamb mince and cook until brown. *This mixture should be reasonably dry; cook out any residue liquid.*

Roll out the dough to around 35 by 20cm (14 by 8in) rectangles and set them onto the hotplate or a heated pan with olive oil.

Spoon a light layer of lamb mix over half of 2 doughs, and spinach mix over half of the others, leaving an inch free around the edge. Fold the rectangles in the middle, covering the filling, and press down on the edges to make the dough stick. *If you need to cook in batches, that's no problem.*

Watch closely, cooking slowly for 4 to 5 minutes on each side. The dough will crisp up, indicating they are ready. *Notice the edges change colour for extra insurance.*

Slice and serve with lemon wedges and hummus (page 214).

LAMB GYROS

Could anything be better than slices of rotisserie-cooked lamb on flatbread with tomatoes, onions, lettuce and tzatziki? Only if you're enjoying it around a campfire with some good company!

This recipe is a real crowd favourite and an easy way to cook for a group. I don't use plates but wrap each gyros in baking paper, so the clean-up is minimal.

2kg of deboned lamb
shoulder

2 cups of extra virgin
olive oil

7 cloves of garlic,
crushed

1 tablespoon each of
salt and pepper

2 tablespoons of
dried oregano

1 tablespoon of dried
rosemary

1 teaspoon of paprika

juice of 1 lemon

a bunch of fresh
rosemary

flatbread (page 230)

tzatziki (page 215)

GREEK SALAD

3 deseeded tomatoes,
cut into wedges

1 telegraph
cucumber, sliced

1 red onion, cut into
moon slices

200g of Kalamata
pitted olives

100g of feta

1 tablespoon of
oregano

extra virgin olive oil

Using a sharp knife, trim excess fat from the lamb. Cut the lamb into 1 to 1.5cm (0.5in) slices, with each piece slightly shorter than a gyros disc, approximately 15cm (6in) across. *It's important that the pieces are evenly sized, or it will disrupt the rotisserie and cook unevenly.*

In a large mixing bowl, combine 1 cup of olive oil, 6 cloves of crushed garlic with the ground pepper, salt, oregano, rosemary, and paprika. Rub the mixture into the meat and let it marinate in the fridge for at least 3 or 4 hours, ideally overnight.

Get a campfire going so there's a nice bed of coals to cook with, or if you use charcoal chimneys, 2 loads are perfect to start with.

With the rotisserie skewer facing up and a gyros disc fitted, push each cut of meat down to the disc. Continue threading the lamb until all meat is stacked as evenly as possible in a criss-cross pattern. Fit the top disc on and tighten it firmly.

Set the spit so the meat is at about the height you can only keep your hand there for 2 to 4 seconds and leave the lamb to rotate continuously for an hour.

Prepare a basting mixture of 1 cup of olive oil, a crushed garlic clove and lemon juice. Brush it on the meat every 20 minutes with the rosemary brush.

While you wait, prepare your flatbread dough and let it rest. Make the tzatziki and combine all the salad ingredients.

When the outside of the lamb is cooked, stop the spit (you may need to raise it if it's too hot), shave off some lamb with a sharp knife, and catch it in a dish.

Slap the dough on the coals below the spit and cook each side for 2 minutes, then brush with olive oil. Alternatively, cook in an oiled skillet over medium-high heat.

Build your gyros. Tear off some baking paper, put a flatbread on top, spoon on tzatziki, add lamb and salad, then wrap and enjoy!

Put the spit back over the coals, brush the lamb with the rosemary, and cut off more meat every 15 minutes until you've eaten so much delicious lamb that you can't walk!

The marinade is perfect for 2kg of meat, but it'll stretch to 4kg if you're feeding 8 to 10 people. Any extra cooked meat can be frozen and enjoyed later. I love bibimbap which isn't very traditional with lamb, but it works so well once coated in gochujang sauce sitting over rice with a dripping egg and lots of veggies like cucumber and carrots.

MOROCCAN LAMB

I'm not the best at expressing myself with words, so if I ever cook you my lamb, it's me sending you a big warm hug. Lamb is my love language. The way the meat falls from the bone and becomes succulent under pressure is divine. This one pairs perfectly with my charred dukkah carrots, which are simple to prepare as the lamb cooks. A nice bottle of cab sav will wash this down perfectly.

2kg of lamb shoulder

extra virgin olive oil

1 tablespoon of salt

1 teaspoon of cracked pepper

1 onion, diced

3 - 4 cloves of garlic

1 carrot, chopped

1 cup of vegetable stock

1 tablespoon of tomato paste

200g of Sicilian olives

½ teaspoon of cardamom pods

2 teaspoons of smokey paprika

1 cinnamon stick

1 teaspoon of cumin

½ teaspoon of turmeric

2 cups of water

crushed pistachios

labneh, (page 203)

dukkah carrots (page 200)

CARAMELISED ONIONS

3 medium brown onions, sliced into moons

2 tablespoons of unsalted butter

1 tablespoon of balsamic vinegar

Let the lamb come to room temperature for about an hour, then use a paper towel to dry it before cooking.

Prepare a bed of coals away from your main fire and place a grate above it so you can cook in a camp oven over medium-high heat – *hot enough that you can only hold your hand 10cm above the cooking surface for 3 to 5 seconds.* If you don't have a grate, put your camp oven straight on the coals, but be more mindful of temperature control.

When the lamb and coals are ready, oil and season the meat with salt and pepper, place it in your preheated camp oven and begin browning, ensuring you turn the meat regularly. Once a nice crust and colour have formed, add the chopped onion, garlic, and carrots and let them sweat for a few minutes.

Deglaze the pot with stock and tomato paste and ensure the liquid covers the meat. *If you pour in just a little of the stock first, its rapid boil will help release the yummy, caramelised bits on the bottom.*

Add the olives and spices. Give it a stir to combine; the sauce will thicken, and the aromas will start filling the air. Add the water and put the lid on.

Move about 70 per cent of the coals from under the camp oven to the lid for a medium simmer. *This is just a guide; the most important thing is maintaining the medium simmer. I like to get my ear next to the camp oven and listen for a gentle bubble and then regulate the coals to maintain it.*

Check after 30 minutes and an hour, topping up the liquid if it's reduced below a quarter of the lamb's height. After the hour check, don't add any more liquid, but keep cooking until all of it has reduced and the meat is falling off the bone. That's usually another 45 minutes to an hour.

Around 20 minutes before the meat's cooked, slowly heat a skillet to medium-high heat. Braise the onions in butter, continuously moving them with a wooden spoon until soft. Drizzle in the balsamic vinegar, and continue mixing while the onions get sticky and golden. They're done when they start to clump together.

When the lamb is ready, serve it on labneh (or thick Greek yoghurt) with caramelised onions and a sprinkle of pistachios alongside charred dukkah carrots.

You can cook this in an oven as well. Once you've followed the steps above until the lid goes on, cook it at 180°C (350°F) for 2 hours.

HOT HONEY PEPPERONI PIZZA

There's nothing like pizza night, and our whole family loves it. We enjoy this special evening once a week, wherever we are on the road, and I start fermenting my dough around 48 hours before. I know, I know, it's a little bit of pre-planning, but good pizza takes time. Fermentation is the key to a decent dough, and it's the way to achieve that beautiful, soft crust with air pockets that bubble up. You can still get a decent result with a 24-hour ferment, but the real magic happens with the double rise. We let the whole dough ball complete the first rise for 24 hours in the fridge or a cool environment, then pull it out, make our dough balls, and let the second rise happen in the fridge for another 24 hours. Then, to make it next level, we drizzle it with hot spicy honey. I must warn you; this is about to change your pizza-eating life!

---

pizza dough
 (page 236)

2 cups of good
 quality honey

3 - 4 habaneros, diced

a 400g tin of Italian
 tomatoes

200g of fresh
 mozzarella

200g of freshly grated
 parmesan

150g of pepperoni,
 sliced

Two days before pizza day, prepare my pizza dough - *trust me, it's worth it.*

On pizza day, preheat your pizza oven or barbecue as hot as it goes. *For the best results in a barbecue, use a pizza stone.* Bring dough balls to room temperature an hour before use.

Pour honey into a saucepan over medium-low heat, gently simmer and be careful not to let it boil. Stir in diced habaneros and gently simmer for 5 minutes, infusing the honey. Strain it into a jar. When cool, seal with an airtight lid.

Using your hands, stretch the pizza dough and shape it. I do this by using my fists and by flipping over the top of my hand and spinning it to make the desired size - my dough recipe should make 4 14in pizzas.

Meanwhile, crush the tinned tomatoes in a bowl and set aside.

Dust a surface with flour, place the dough down and cover the centre of the pizza with the tomatoes using the back of a spoon.

Arrange mozzarella and parmesan over the tomato sauce, then spread on the pepperoni. Cook in your pizza oven until the cheese blisters. Slice and serve with a generous drizzle of hot honey.

Stretch each pizza dough ball one at a time and keep the others covered to prevent them from drying out as you make and cook your pizzas.

PULLED PORK TACOS

I quickly learnt how to turn one meal into many while living in my little Kombi van, mostly due to our fridge space. Pulled pork is so succulent and versatile that I can stretch it over three or four meals. We always start with tacos, then burgers, quesadillas, and pulled pork eggs benny. When we last headed through the middle of Australia, it got us all the way from the Flinders Ranges to Uluru.

2kg of boneless pork shoulder

sea salt and black pepper

extra virgin olive oil

1 tablespoon of paprika

2 tablespoons of cayenne pepper

1 tablespoon of cumin

$\frac{1}{2}$ cup of honey

$\frac{1}{3}$ cup of apple cider vinegar

2 cups of vegetable stock

$\frac{2}{3}$ cup of pineapple juice

1 onion, quartered

3 cloves of garlic

slaw (page 206)

200g tin of chipotle in adobo sauce

8 corn or flour tortillas (page 232)

fresh coriander and chilli

Prepare a bed of coals away from your main fire and place a grate above it so you can cook in a camp oven over medium-high heat – *hot enough that you can only hold your hand 10cm above the cooking surface for 3 to 5 seconds.*

Cover the pork in salt and pepper, rubbing with olive oil before searing each side in the camp oven for 3 to 5 minutes, or until golden.

Meanwhile, mix the spices, honey, apple cider vinegar, stock and half the pineapple juice in a bowl and give it a big stir. Pour the mixture over the seared pork so that half is submerged. Add water if it's not. Add the onions and whole garlic cloves and put the lid on.

Move about 70 per cent of the coals from under the camp oven to the lid for a medium simmer. *This is just a guide; the most important thing is maintaining the medium simmer. I like to get my ear next to the camp oven and listen for a gentle bubble and then regulate the coals to maintain it.*

At around 30-minute intervals, check on the liquid content. If the liquid is below the halfway mark at the 1 hour check, top it up with water. After this, you shouldn't need to add any more.

Meanwhile, make the slaw and whip up a batch of chipotle sauce by combining the chipotle and half the pineapple juice.

After 3 to 4 hours, you will have a succulent and soft pot of meat. It's ready when it can be pulled apart with 2 forks.

There will be plenty of leftover pulled pork for other meals, so take what you need for the tacos, drain the excess liquid with a slotted spoon, place it in a bowl and mix chipotle sauce through.

Warm up tortillas for 2 minutes on each side, then add pork, slaw and, fresh coriander and chilli. Serve with a wedge of lime.

To store the pork for leftovers, drain the juice into a jar and place the pork in a separate container. Each time you reheat, add some of the juice so the pork always stays beautiful and hydrated. I love to overcook the pork a little when I fry it back up, so it has delicious burnt ends throughout.

PREP: 20 MIN   COOK: 40 MINS   SERVES: 2-6

YAKITORI

I met Lockie in Auckland. He was a pilot at the airline I was a flight attendant for. We were inseparable, escaping on weekends at any opportunity. I'd found my wanderlust soul mate. As our relationship blossomed, he got the dream opportunity to move to Japan. We packed our home, said our goodbyes, and spent the next six years in Tokyo, full of vibrance, history, culture and tradition.

I immersed myself in Japanese cuisine, exploring the streets of Tokyo while he went through training. Each day I set out to discover new flavours and experiences. Japanese culture insists on perfection, which extends to its food. Many Japanese chefs have spent their entire life perfecting a single cuisine using recipes passed down through generations.

There, we discovered yakitori (yaki – grilled and tori – chicken). In front of a little hole-in-the-wall vendor with an open grill smoking away, we'd line up for the garlic clove and chicken thigh, traditionally served with a tare (marinade) sauce or doused with shio (salt). The flavours from the white charcoal as the skewers are gently and continuously turned to develop a salty, smoky flavour with softly caramelised garlic. Ah, the nostalgia.

As we travelled Australia, we craved this timelessly simple stick and decided to try it ourselves. We discovered yakitori is the perfect camping meal and can be cooked over a bed of coals, a hibachi grill, BBQ or a pan. Now I can bring the flavours of Japan around the campfire with a few simple ingredients and a large cold Asahi. Kanpai!

The recipe below is the yakitori that we enjoy, but feel free to get adventurous here and add whatever vegetables or other meats you like. The method remains the same.

bamboo skewers

700g of free-range
   chicken thigh

2 large garlic bulbs

1 bunch of spring
   onion

salt

TARE SAUCE

$\frac{1}{2}$ cup of mirin

$\frac{1}{4}$ cup of sake

$\frac{1}{2}$ cup of soy sauce

$\frac{1}{2}$ cup water

$\frac{1}{2}$ cup of brown sugar

2 cloves of garlic,
   grated

1 tablespoon of
   freshly grated
   ginger

We like to use a hibachi grill, but you can repare a bed of coals and place a grate above it so you can cook over medium-high heat – *hot enough that you can only hold your hand 10cm above the cooking surface for 3 to 5 seconds.. We love using Japanese binchotan charcoal, but this is not a requirement.* While the coals are heating up, soak the bamboo skewers for 20 minutes.

Meanwhile, whip up a tare sauce. Combine the mirin, sake, soy sauce, water, brown sugar, garlic, and ginger in a saucepan or billy. Bring the sauce to a boil, then reduce the heat to a simmer.

Let it simmer for about 20 minutes until the sauce has reduced by half and is thick like sticky syrup. *It should coat the back of a spoon without dripping straight off.* Strain to remove the garlic and ginger, then pour it into a dipping bowl or jar.

While the sauce is simmering - slice the chicken into 2cm (1in) thick pieces. Peel the garlic, but keep the cloves whole. Cut the spring onion into 2cm lengths.

On half the sticks, thread on chicken, with a whole piece of garlic between each bit. On the other sticks, do the same, but use the spring onion pieces. Season with salt.

Cook the skewers directly over the coals on your grate, turning frequently for 15 to 20 minutes until cooked. The smoke slowly infuses the skewers and reduces the burn by continuous turns. *If you want a more smoky flavour, fan the coals with a piece of cardboard or your hat.*

Once cooked, dip each skewer in tare sauce and place them back on the grill for a minute, turning quickly. Repeat 2 or 3 times to caramelise the sauce and shape its beautiful flavour.

Just like on the streets of Japan, eat them straight off the stick with big handles of beer.

KARAAGE CHICKEN

SERVES: 4-6

COOK: 10 MINS

PREP: 1-2 HOURS

Riley lives for "crunchy" chicken. I would be lying if I didn't say I wasn't partial to some myself. Karaage is a fun and simple Japanese-style entree often found in izakaya's (Japanese pubs). It is the juiciest and tenderest fried chicken you'll find.

I learnt this method while living in Japan, playing in my little kitchen, but this is a great dish to cook over the fire or on gas.

700 - 800g of skinless chicken thighs (about 6)

1 tablespoon of finely grated fresh ginger

2 tablespoons of soy sauce

2 tablespoons of cooking sake

1 tablespoon of mirin

1 litre of vegetable or rice bran oil, for frying

2 cups katakuriko (Japanese potato starch)

sea salt

1 lemon, quartered

2 tablespoons of Kewpie mayonnaise

Dice the chicken into 2 to 3cm (1in) pieces.

In a large bowl, combine the ginger, soy sauce, sake and mirin, then add the chicken, ensuring they are well coated. Leave it to marinate for a minimum of 1 to 2 hours. The longer, the better.

Fill a wok or deep pot with oil about 4cm (1.5in) deep until it reaches a temperature of around 160°C (320°F). *I check the temperature by putting the opposite end of a wooden spoon in – you should see oil steadily bubbling around the wood.*

Pat the chicken lightly with paper towel to remove any excess moisture – it helps the batter stick rather than dripping off – before dunking it into the starch. Turn to coat well.

The chicken gets double-fried – it's browned in oil, drained, and then fried again to crunchy perfection. Fry it in batches for 2 to 3 minutes, then drain the oil from the chicken by placing it on scrunched-up paper towel while you cook the rest.

Once it's all cooked, skim any debris out of the oil and then increase the heat to around 190°C (375°F) for the second fry. *Use the wooden spoon test – the bubbles should be larger and rise quicker.* Refry the chicken for 2 minutes or until it's crispy and golden.

Sprinkle with sea salt and serve with a lemon wedge and Kewpie.

You can find katakuriko in any Asian supermarket, but if not, any potato, corn or even tapioca starch will work. This batter is also terrific for calamari. If you've got leftover chicken, a karaage chicken wrap loaded with Kewpie mayo and cabbage is a great lunchbox filler.

CHICKEN TAGINE

Morocco has always fascinated me. There's something magical about its food, the spices, the snake charmers, and Moroccan cooks' incredible ability to blend savoury, sweet, and sour flavours. We went a few years ago and spent five days exploring the souks in downtown Marrakech. I came home with a passion for cooking with a tagine. I find it incredible how the cone-shaped lid circulates the steam and brings moisture back down to the food, making each bite so tender.

$\frac{1}{2}$ teaspoon of ground ginger

1 teaspoon of paprika

$\frac{1}{2}$ teaspoon of ground cumin

$\frac{1}{2}$ teaspoon of turmeric

$\frac{1}{2}$ teaspoon of cardamom pods, crushed

1 cinnamon stick

salt and black pepper

4 tablespoons of extra virgin olive oil, plus extra for frying

1kg of skin-on chicken thighs

1 brown onion, diced

3 cloves of garlic, finely chopped

180g of pitted green olives

1 cup of chicken stock

juice and rind of half a lemon

lemon couscous (page 199)

slithered almonds and flat-leaf parsley, to garnish

This recipe will also work in a camp oven if you don't have a tagine. Be sure to leave the skin on the chicken; it prevents it from drying out and helps release its beautiful organic flavouring. Prepare the spice rub and allow the chicken to marinate overnight for a more intense flavour. Traditionally, tagines have lots of dried and preserved fruit, so if you have any in your cupboard, throw them in. You can also swap the fresh lemons for preserved ones.

Prepare a bed of coals away from your main fire and use 2 rocks or a grate to suspend your tagine over medium heat – *hot enough that you can only hold your hand 10cm above the cooking surface for 6 to 8 seconds.*

While that's settling in, combine all the spices and olive oil in a mixing bowl. Add the chicken and use your hands to rub the marinade all over until the chicken is completely covered.

Sear the chicken pieces, skin down, in some olive oil for 3 to 5 minutes. Once they're lovely and brown, add the onions and garlic and let them soften for 3 to 4 minutes.

Spread the olives around and add 2 slithers of lemon rind, the lemon juice and the stock (or as much as you need to cover the chicken). With the lid on, bring it to a boil. Listen to the tagine. Once boiling, reduce the coals to maintain a gentle simmer for 45 minutes to an hour. Check after 25 minutes, and if all the liquid has reduced, add more stock or water.

While that's cooking, prepare a batch of my lemon couscous.

It's ready when the chicken falls apart. Serve over the couscous with fresh parsley and slithered almonds.

CHAPTER 4

SEAFOOD

This chapter is an ode to my simple love and adoration for kaimoana – seafood.
I want it to inspire you to try something new with your next catch or fresh buy.
Over the following pages, I have added some of my favourite share methods,
techniques I have grown up with and recipes that my travels have inspired.

LET'S TALK ABOUT FISH

Fishing was always a big part of my life growing up.
I can't think of many weekends as a child that didn't involve
fishing or the beach. Now older and with my own children,
I love watching them enjoy the ocean, just as I did.

There's something so rewarding about catch and cook, taking
only what we need and using as much of the fish as we can.
When travelling, we always have our little inflatable boat with
us wherever we go and head out often, enjoying these special
moments with big smiles when we bring home some dinner.

In Australia and New Zealand we are spoiled with some
exceptional fish. I grew up with tarakihi, snapper, kahawai
(Australian salmon) and kingfish. But it wasn't until we travelled
Australia that I discovered some of my absolute favourite fish.

CORAL TROUT

If there were only one fish I could eat for the rest of my life, this would be it. These beautiful fish are found in the northern half of Australia and have a firm, luscious white flesh with a lovely, sweet flavour. I love it raw in dishes like my Coconut Habanero Raw Fish as much as I love to cook them whole over coals. The skin crisps up beautifully, and it marries perfectly with the smoky flavours from the charcoal. Coral trout is one fish that you don't want to waste a single part of, and the wings and cheeks offer some of the sweetest meat around.

NANNYGAI

Also known as red snapper or bight redfish, this is a prized fish found in southern waters and up the east coast of Australia. It's a great all-round fish and is fantastic raw and in ceviche due to its lovely white flesh and mildly sweet flavour. One of our favourite places in Australia is the Eyre Peninsula. There's incredible camping, people, seafood and jaw-dropping beaches. But another big plus for this region is the healthy population of nannygai. When on the Eyre, it's what we love to eat, accompanied by a few Coffin Bay oysters, of course!

BARRAMUNDI

A great Aussie icon. Low in fat and high in omega 3, this is a nice, healthy fish that I like to use in curries. It stands up well to spices and takes on flavour beautifully. It's also great pan-fried with crispy skin.

SNAPPER

The humble snapper is probably the most versatile fish around. If you are hesitant about seafood, this is a great place to start. You can find it just about everywhere throughout Australia and New Zealand, and the flesh is moist, mildly sweet and loves citrus. Snapper fairs extremely well raw, crumbed, floured and battered. My grandmother smothers it in lemon pepper and chucks it on the BBQ for an easy crowd-pleaser.

SALMON

Grilled, baked or as sashimi; salmon is a class act, and for my little girl Alba, the pink fish brings her so much joy. It is a fantastic fish to smoke or cover a whole side in lemon slices, wrap in foil and chuck directly on the coals. I also love adding hot-smoked salmon to my fish pie (page 154) as it gives the whole dish a lot of flavour.

CHILLI & GARLIC FISH TACOS

A fish taco is something that I think nearly everyone has a soft spot for. They are quick, easy, and perfect beachside on a lovely afternoon with a cold beer. They are definitely on the top of the list every time we catch fresh fish.

1 red onion, cut into half moons

a pinch of flaky salt

$\frac{1}{3}$ cup water

$\frac{1}{3}$ cup vinegar

juice of 1 lime

1 tablespoon of mixed peppercorns

100g of unsalted butter

2 garlic cloves, crushed

3 tablespoons of lemon juice

350g or 4 fillets of white fish, diced roughly 2cm (1in)

6 flour tortillas

$\frac{1}{2}$ a red cabbage, finely sliced

1 long red chilli, deseeded and finely sliced, for garnishing

a bunch of coriander

SALSA VERDE

$\frac{1}{2}$ a green capsicum

1 jalapeño

a bunch of coriander

a bunch of flat-leaf parsley

2 cloves of garlic, crushed and chopped

1 onion, finely diced

3 tinned tomatillos

3 tablespoons of olive oil

2 tablespoons of lime or lemon juice

flaky salt

Pickling onions is easy. Toss them in a bowl and season with salt and add the water and vinegar. Squeeze the lime juice over the top to taste. Set aside while you prepare the rest.

Start on the salsa verde. Blister the capsicum and jalapeno over a flame until well blackened. Place them into a bowl and cover for 5 minutes to allow them to sweat.

Meanwhile, finely chop the herbs and place them into a bowl with the chopped garlic and onion. Chop the tinned tomatillos and add them, too.

Rub the blackened skin off the capsicum and jalapeno with your fingers. *Don't be too fussy here; some blackened bits add a nice flavour to the salsa.* Roughly chop and add to the mixture. Drizzle olive oil and lime juice into the bowl and give it all a generous mix. Season with flaky salt and leave it with the onions.

Over medium-high heat, add peppercorns to a skillet and cook until fragrant (about 2 minutes). Tip them into a mortar and pestle, or crush them with the side of a knife.

In a skillet, soften the garlic in butter and add the peppercorns until the butter foams, then squeeze in the lemon juice. Add the fish into the skillet and spoon the butter over the top consistently until the fish turns completely white. Remove from the heat.

Warm your tortillas for 20 seconds on each side straight over the flame or in a skillet. Build the tacos on the warm tortillas with cabbage, fish, pickled onions, chilli and coriander. Serve with limes and salsa verde.

I like snapper, nannygai, or coral trout, but any fish will work fine. I am, pretty much, always a corn tortilla girl, but flour tortillas work well for this recipe – they are softer and more forgiving. Adjust or omit the chilli if it's too spicy for you.

NORM'S SEAFOOD CHOWDER

Whenever we would visit Lockie's grandfather, as tradition we would call into his local fish shop and pick up fresh seafood for my chowder, a dish he really enjoyed. I would hear him chat to friends and family over the phone, telling them how he loved it because it was served in a little roll. It's beautiful how a good seafood chowder can make you feel, it warms your soul.

50g of butter

1 white onion, finely diced

3 cloves of garlic, finely chopped

1 leek, finely sliced

1 carrot, finely diced

2 level tablespoons of plain flour

$\frac{1}{2}$ cup of cream

3 cups of fish or chicken stock

150g of snapper or whitefish

150g of skinless salmon

10-12 green prawns, peeled and deveined

2 calamari tubes, cut into rings

10-12 mussels in shells, de-bearded and well-scrubbed

4 bowl-sized round sourdough loaves

salt and cracked pepper, to season

$\frac{1}{4}$ cup of parsley, finely chopped

$\frac{1}{4}$ cup of chives to serve, chopped

$\frac{1}{2}$ cup of lemon juice

With skinless salmon, err on the side of caution as it can quickly overcook. I recommend adding it in the last 3 to 5 minutes if you like it rare. Pick up your fish stock from your local fishmonger; they often make it fresh.

Prepare a bed of coals away from your main fire and place a grate above it so you can cook in a camp oven over medium heat – *hot enough that you can only hold your hand 10cm above the cooking surface for 6 to 8 seconds.*

Add half the butter, then onion, garlic, leek, and carrot and sauté, stirring occasionally until softened, then push to the outside of the pot.

Place the rest of the butter in the centre of the pot, sprinkle flour over the butter, and, using a wooden spoon, quickly cook the flour into the butter until golden (be careful not to overcook it). It should take around 45 seconds. Add the cream and stir until it's smooth with no flour lumps. Pour in the stock and stir as it gently simmers and thickens for 8 to 10 minutes.

Begin folding in the fish, prawns, calamari, and mussels. Pop a lid on for 10 minutes to allow the seafood to cook.

Meanwhile, warm bread rolls on your grate, then scoop the inside from them to make a bowl.

When the seafood is cooked, remove it from the heat, spoon the chowder into warmed bread rolls, and season with salt and pepper. Add parsley and chives on top with a squeeze of lemon juice.

WHOLE CORAL TROUT

Something magic happens when coral trout is cooked whole, over coals. It rewards you with meat that's soft, smoky and sweet. The skin crisps up beautifully and can almost resemble pork crackle. The cheeks and wings are also incredibly delicious. The entire experience of cooking and enjoying this fish whole is so good; I find it hard to put into words.

1.5 – 2.5kg coral trout, gutted, gilled and scaled

4 tablespoons of flaky sea salt

$\frac{1}{3}$ cup of extra virgin olive oil, preferably in a spray bottle

2 lemons

rotisserie skewer and prongs (these are really easy to find at any barbecue store)

2 y-shaped branches (long enough to dig into the sand and ensure the fish is stable, roughly 70cm)

Get a campfire going so there's a nice bed of coals to use. *I'll often use lump charcoal for this meal - about 3 charcoal chimneys full.* Meanwhile, set the coral trout aside and bring it to room temperature for about 20 minutes, then pat it dry with a tea towel or paper towel.

While the fire and fish are coming up to temperature, dig Y-shaped branches in the sand near, but not over, the fire, and make sure the Y's line up about 40cm high and are level.

With 1 prong fitted to the skewer, pierce the fish through the mouth and run it below the spine and out through the tail. *It will require some force when exiting the tail.* Fit the second prong tightly to secure the fish. Salt the fish generously on each side and pat the salt in.

Lay a bed of coals between the Y branches. You need enough so that you can only hold your hand at fish-cooking height for 2 to 4 seconds. Adjust coals to maintain this.

Place fish on Y branches with belly down for first 5 minutes, then turn the fish 90° and repeat every 5 minutes for 45 to 60 minutes of total cooking time. *You might need to manoeuvre the fish so that 1 of the prong clips is in the Y branch to keep it from turning itself over.* Every time you turn, gently spray the fish with olive oil, and you will start to see the skin bubble and turn golden. That's a great sign.

The fish is cooked when the flesh is pearly white and flaky. If you've got a meat thermometer, the internal temperature should read 48°C (118°F). Once it's cooked, remove it from the heat, take out the skewer and forks, and let it rest for 10 minutes.

Serve on newspaper (like when we were kids), sitting around a fire with a big squeeze of lemon juice and my zucchini salad from page 193.

Coral trout is a fish that doesn't need extra flavour, so I simply rub it with salt flakes before cooking, spray it with extra virgin olive oil a few times during the cook, and then a big squeeze of lemon juice once done. This fish really does speak for itself.

WASABI-SEARED TUNA BOWLS

We all loved the Northern Territory. We left no stone unturned, and that meant a visit to Arnhem Land – a 13-hour bumpy drive from Katherine. Yet, beaming with excitement, the rich red dirt, blue seas, and Yolngu people blew us away.

With two weeks of exploring and camping ahead, we decided to hire a boat to see the outer islands. It was a beautiful day on the water, and the kids were having loads of fun watching schools of jumping tuna right at the nose of our boat. The next minute the fight was on, and we lured in our first one. That night I made my wasabi-seared tuna bowls, an easy and fresh dish with simple ingredients. I also prepped the kid's tuna kebabs to enjoy. We moved on from Arnhem Land with heavy hearts, to be honest we could have stayed there for months. It was a very special place.

350g of fresh tuna

1 cucumber

$\frac{1}{2}$ a red onion, sliced

1 teaspoon of sugar

$\frac{1}{4}$ cup of rice wine vinegar

2 tablespoons of wasabi

$\frac{1}{2}$ cup of light, salt-reduced soy sauce

1 cup of sesame seeds

2 cups of brown rice

1 tablespoon of pickled ginger

1 cup of edamame

2 tablespoons of ponzu sauce

$\frac{1}{2}$ a red chilli

Get a campfire going so there's a nice bed of coals. Meanwhile, set the tuna aside and bring it to room temperature.

Using a potato peeler, peel cucumber ribbons and slice the red onion. Put it in a jar with the sugar and rice wine vinegar (save a teaspoon to mix through the rice later), then leave it to sit. Mix the wasabi and soy sauce in a mixing bowl to make a paste.

Spread out the sesame seeds on a board and roll the tuna steak through the paste before coating it in the sesame seeds. Set it aside.

Wash the rice until the water runs clear. Cook the rice for 15 to 20 minutes or until it's soft and moist on the outside but still firm and chewy in the middle.

Heat a skillet or hot plate to medium-high heat for searing. *Check with a water droplet – if the water dances, it's hot enough for searing.* Place the tuna steaks on the skillet or hot plate and sear each side for 60 to 90 seconds for medium-rare. *I highly recommend having it as rare as you can handle to ensure it remains tender and succulent rather than tough and dry.*

Remove the steaks once the crust has formed, and let them rest for at least 5 minutes before you slice them.

In the meantime, add a teaspoon of rice wine vinegar to the rice and fluff with a fork. Serve the rice in a bowl with pickled cucumber, onion and ginger, tuna, and edamame. Pour ponzu sauce over the top and add fresh chilli to your liking.

BARRA TIKKA SKEWERS

The beloved barramundi. It's hearty, healthy and tasty. As far as fish goes, barra is the king staple throughout Australia. It has a splendid texture that works so well in the bright spices of tikka, and here lies the reason why I have chosen it to skewer with a mild and rich rub.

1 teaspoon of salt

1 teaspoon of cracked black pepper

$\frac{1}{2}$ teaspoon of turmeric

2 teaspoons of ground coriander

1 teaspoon of ground cumin

1 teaspoon of garam masala

$\frac{1}{3}$ cup of finely diced coriander root

1 teaspoon of smoky paprika

4 cloves of garlic, grated

1 lemongrass stalk, bashed and finely chopped

juice and zest of 1 lime

$\frac{1}{2}$ cup of natural Greek yoghurt

400g of barramundi,

2 tablespoons of extra virgin olive oil

2 teaspoons of ginger, grated

6 soaked bamboo skewers

1 long red chilli

fresh coriander

MINT SAUCE

1 cup of natural Greek yoghurt

$\frac{1}{2}$ cup roughly chopped mint

$\frac{1}{2}$ cup roughly chopped coriander leaves

3 cloves garlic

3 tablespoons lemon juice

salt and pepper to taste

COCONUT RICE

2 cups of jasmine rice

2 cups of coconut water

$\frac{1}{2}$ cup of coconut cream

Combine the spices, garlic, lemongrass and lime zest in a mixing bowl with the lime juice and yoghurt. Cube the barramundi and coat the pieces well with your hands. Let it marinate in the fridge for at least 30 minutes.

While it's marinating, make the mint sauce. Mix the mint, coriander and garlic into the Greek yoghurt until thoroughly combined. Squeeze in the lemon juice and season with salt and pepper. Leave it to sit in the fridge for 20 minutes before serving.

Meanwhile, prepare some coconut rice. Thoroughly wash the rice, then add it to a saucepan with the coconut water and cream. With the lid on, bring it to a simmer and leave it there for 8 to 12 minutes.

Remove the barra from the fridge and thread it evenly onto the skewers. Heat a skillet to medium-high heat and add a splash of olive or coconut oil.

Fry the skewers for 2 minutes on each side. The marinade will get sticky, which I like, but you can splash in more oil if it's getting stuck. Remove once the flesh is firm.

Fluff the rice with a fork and garnish it with chilli sliced and fresh coriander. Serve with coconut rice, mint yoghurt and naan bread, and poppadums if you have them.

COCONUT HABANERO RAW FISH

As a child, I remember my grandfather diving and fishing most weekends. If he came home with a tarakihi or snapper, we would have raw fish. The Māori rely on a cured style, with hints of seawater and freshly picked lemons over soft white fish.

Many islands throughout the Pacific have a similar version and you may have experienced it yourself in the Cook Islands, Fiji, Tonga or Samoa. Like every country, each dish is modified by the ingredients in their region or by personal taste. The dish I have for you below is pure indulgence and each piece will melt in your mouth. My recipe draws from our travels throughout Mexico (ceviche), adding chilli and lime and coconut cream like Fiji's kokoda.

500g of fresh white fish like snapper, nannygai or coral trout

1 lemon

2 limes, for juice

1 medium habanero or green chilli

$\frac{1}{2}$ a red onion

$\frac{1}{4}$ of a red capsicum

1 truss tomato, deseeded

400ml of coconut cream

salt and pepper, to taste

Slice the fish into 1in by half-inch slithers and begin layering them into a serving bowl. Squeeze the juice of a lemon and lime over the fish. Set it aside in the fridge.

Blister the habanero over a flame until it's blackened. Put it in a covered bowl to cool; *the steam will allow the skin to peel off easier.*

Meanwhile, thinly dice the red onion, capsicum, and the deseeded truss tomato.

Remove fish from the fridge. It should have started to cure and begun to turn white. Add the red onion, capsicum, and tomato with the fish.

Remove the habanero from the bowl, gently peel the blackened skin off, and remove the seeds if you don't like the heat. *I like it hot, so I leave all the seeds in.* Finely dice habanero, then add it to the fish. Mix in the coconut cream and top with the juice of the second lime. Season to your likening with salt and pepper.

It is ready to be served now, however, I like to let it rest for at least 20 to 30 minutes – I find the flavour is better this way. The longer it sits in the fridge, the softer the fish becomes; this is a favourite the next day. We like to spoon the fish onto corn chips, however, it's also beautiful on its own.

SMOKED FISH PIE

Whenever we are craving a quick one-pan meal, this is what our family will easily choose. It's a great treat to spark up the fire on the beach while the kids build sandcastles and the pan bubbles away. Eat straight from the skillet as the sun goes down.

100g of unsalted butter

1 white onion, diced

2 cloves of crushed garlic

1 carrot diced

$\frac{1}{3}$ cup of fresh tarragon

2 level tablespoons of plain flour

$\frac{1}{2}$ cup of milk

$\frac{1}{2}$ cup of vegetable stock

2 cups of sour cream

200g of firm white fish, diced

200g of hot-smoked salmon fillets

salt and pepper, to taste

2 medium sweet potatoes, skin on

1 cup of grated mild cheese

Prepare a bed of coals away from your main fire and place a grate above it so you can cook in a skillet or camp oven over medium heat – *hot enough that you can only hold your hand 10cm above the cooking surface for 6 to 8 seconds.*

Add half the butter and all the onion, garlic, carrot, and tarragon and sauté, stirring occasionally, until the veggies soften.

Push the sautéed veggies to the outside of the pot and add the rest of the butter in the centre. Sprinkle flour over the butter, and, using a wooden spoon, quickly cook it into the butter until golden (be careful not to overcook it); this should take around 45 seconds. Add the milk and stir until it's smooth with no lumps of flour.

Pour in the stock and sour cream and continue to stir. Let it gently simmer and thicken for 8 to 10 minutes.

Begin folding in the fish and flaking the salmon, and season well with salt and pepper.

Thinly slice rounds of sweet potato and arrange them evenly around the top of the fish mixture. Sprinkle with cheese.

Place camp oven lid on and add a light layer of coals on top to crust the sweet potato. *You'll need less if using a skillet rather than a camp oven. Keep a very close eye on it, as it's easy to burn the sweet potatoes if it's too hot.*

Best served beachside.

Use leftovers to make smoked fish croquettes. Roll the cooled, leftover mixture into balls and set it in the fridge. Add breadcrumbs and grated parmesan cheese, egg wash and flour to three bowls and roll the balls into the flour, followed by the egg, and finish with crumbs. Cook in hot rice bran oil around three-quarters full in a wok. Cook until golden.

CRAYFISH
AND ME

I was raised in a fishing and diving family on the east coast of New Zealand, so I was spoiled to have have grown up eating crayfish my whole life.

As a little girl, I remember waiting on the beach for my grandad to come in from diving to see what he had caught. He'd never take more than he needed, just what was enough to feed our family. As kids, we'd get the legs to share and compete to see who could get the longest bits out without breaking them.

But growing up, we had crayfish served only one way – boiled in saltwater. Don't get me wrong, it is still one of my favourite ways to enjoy these beautiful delicacies, but as we

grew older, my sister and I would often experiment with different dishes and ways of cooking them.

Australia is home to four main species of crayfish – eastern, southern, western, and tropical. While all are incredible, for me, it's the southern rock lobster that gels perfectly with my tastebuds. We have the same species back home in New Zealand (*Jasus edwardsii*), although we call them reds. They are so flavourful with silky, creamy flesh that is perfect to steam or barbecue with a little butter, or even for sashimi.

Over the years, I've picked up some simple handling and cooking techniques and recipes perfect for crayfish. I've shared them here.

Handling Live Crays

Crayfish must be dispatched in the most humane way possible. Chilling them between 0 and 4°C degrees for a minimum of 20 minutes slows their nervous system and makes them insensible. The best way to do this is by placing them in a saltwater ice slurry (three parts ice to one part seawater). If you don't have access to seawater, add 35g (two tablespoons) of salt to a litre of water. If you don't have ice, use a freezer, but it will take longer for them to cool enough to become insensible before they can be dispatched. Crayfish have two nerve centres and can be most effectively dispatched by quickly cutting them in half lengthways, starting with the head.

Halving Crayfish

With the crayfish on its back, insert a long, sharp knife between its eyes and push the blade down to the board. Flip the crayfish over to expose the underside and cut straight down the centre from head to tail. Remove the black shoot and any other stomach material.

Removing the tail

To remove the tail, hold the body in one hand, insert a knife into where the tail meets the head, and run it all around the outside. There is a membrane here we want to free before pulling the tail. Then holding the body with one hand and the head with the other, twist, and the tail should come away with all the meat attached from the head.

Removing the tail meat

With scissors, cut straight down each side of the belly towards the tail.

Start at the top and use your fingers to get right in between the shell and the meat, and it should peel away nice and easy, all the way to the tail. Then remove the black shoot.

You can remove the raw tail meat from the shell, but it's much easier if you boil or steam the tails for a minute and then pull it out. That doesn't cook the meat much, but it makes it far easier to separate from the shell.

The Head and Legs

If you're using just the tail, never discard the head, as it's one of the most beautiful parts of the crayfish. The head is where you find the mustard, my grandad's favourite part. If I'm just using the tail, I will always boil the rest of the crayfish and get stuck right into the legs. You can also make a crayfish bisque or a good seafood stock from them.

Frozen Crays

In a fridge, let crayfish thaw in a covered dish for 18-24 hours.

Crayfish flesh is delicate and sensitive to temperature changes. Water thawing and other quick thaw methods can spoil your them.

Steaming Crays

Steaming is the best way to cook crayfish to preserve most of their natural flavour and tenderness.

In the bottom of a large pot, add two inches of seawater or salted water (35g of salt per litre of water) and with a steaming rack or double boiler in place, bring the water to a boil over high heat.

Add the crayfish one at a time and don't overcrowd them, then put the lid on and start timing. After a few minutes, I like to lift the lid and move the crayfish around so they cook evenly.

Crayfish is cooked when the shell turns bright orange and the flesh is white and firm. Cook time will depend on weight but use this as a rough guide:

500 to 700g	**8 – 13 minutes**
800g to 1kg	**14 – 18 minutes**
1.1 kg to 1.5kg	**19 – 32 minutes**
1.6kg to 2kg	**33 – 40 minutes**

Immediately after the crays have finished cooking, put them in ice or cold water to arrest the cooking process.

Boiling Crays

In a large pot, bring seawater or salted water (35g of salt per litre of water) to a boil over high heat, then add the crayfish. Once the pot begins to boil again, cook the crays for about eight to 12 minutes or until the shell turns bright orange. The time is dependent on crayfish size, but I always cook for eight minutes as a minimum.

Immediately after the crays have finished cooking, put them in ice or cold water to arrest the cooking process. When cooled, rest the crays vertically with the tail up to let any excess water drain. I snap the antennas, which helps drain them faster and, I believe, results in nicer-tasting meat.

Cooked crayfish can be stored in a fridge for up to three days or frozen for up to two months.

Barbecuing Crays

Heat a barbecue to medium heat and halve the crayfish, removing the shoot and stomach material. Brush the flesh with butter or oil and place them, meat down, on the grill for three minutes. Flip them and brush again with butter, then grill for another two to three minutes or until the flesh turns white and firm.

MANGO SALSA CRAYFISH CUPS

This simple and delightful recipe encapsulates this highly loved crustacean's true textures and flavours. I have paired it with zest, sweet mango and fresh herbs. It's a perfect crowd pleaser or for beachside dinners with a glass of sav!

the meat of 1 cooked crayfish tail

1 large, ripe but firm mango

1 bunch of coriander

2 baby cos lettuce heads

1 spring onion, white part sliced

DRESSING

$\frac{1}{4}$ cup of water

2 tablespoons of sugar

1 $\frac{1}{2}$ tablespoons of lime juice

2 tablespoons of fish sauce

1 red chilli, finely chopped

Start with the zesty dressing. Add water and sugar to a bowl and mix until the sugar dissolves, then add the lime juice and fish sauce. Add enough chilli to suit your preference for heat.

Cut the crayfish meat into bite-size pieces (about 2cm/1in) and place them into a bowl. Dice the mango flesh, add it to the crayfish with the coriander and gently toss it all together.

Lay cleaned cos lettuce leaves on a platter and fill each cup with the crayfish mix, then drizzle over the dressing, finishing with some finely chopped spring onion to garnish.

SIMPLE PRAWN BAO COCKTAILS

One of our favourite traditions on the Gold Coast is to stop past the prawn trawlers and grab a few bags of sweet, fresh prawns. Most of the time, we buy double – peeling and eating a dozen right there. It's wonderful to support the local fisherman; they are a good sort and often love a chat. When I'm off to see family or friends, this is my way to impress them without slaving away over a meal.

500g of cooked prawns, peeled and deveined

6 bao buns

1 cos lettuce head

1 jalapeño, sliced

2 tablespoons of coriander

lime wedges

SAUCE

2 tablespoons kewpie

1 tablespoon sriracha sauce

1 tablespoon of lime juice

Mix the kewpie, sriracha and lime juice. Dice the prawns into large chunks and toss the sauce through until evenly coated.

Steam the bao buns for 8 minutes or until soft.

Layer the baos with a lettuce leaf, prawns and sliced jalapeno. Serve with lime wedges

A great appetiser best served with a limey margarita.

FIRE-ROASTED CRAYFISH

There's nothing like a beach fire after a day on the water, so this is one of my favourite ways to cook crayfish when they are super fresh. Whenever we come in with a good feed of crays, we light a fire straight away and cook a few on the beach. Simplicity is often where perfection is found.

200g of salted butter, softened

3 cloves of garlic, grated

a bunch of flat-leaf parsley leaves, picked and chopped

juice and zest of a lemon

1 - 2 crayfish, halved

Prepare garlic and herb butter by grating the garlic into the butter and mixing it with the parsley and lemon zest using a fork.

Place butter mix onto baking paper and roll it into a small log. Fold the paper over and twist the ends like a toffee lolly wrapper. Leave it in the fridge to harden for at least 10 minutes.

While the butter is chilling, prepare your coals and place a grate where you'll have medium-high heat – *hot enough that you can only hold your hand 10cm above the cooking surface for 3 to 5 seconds.*

Remove the butter from the fridge and cut it into half-inch knobs, then evenly place them over the flesh of the crayfish. Place the cray halves onto the grate, meat facing up, and cover with a metal bowl, tray or upside-down camp oven. If you don't have any of these, use foil. Cook for 8 to 10 minutes or until the flesh is white and firm.

Squeeze lemon juice over to finish. Enjoy!

TEMPURA POPCORN CRAYFISH

If you're a fan of popcorn chicken, I have a treat for you! Crunchy crayfish is to die for – it's simple, delicious, and each little morsel melts in your mouth. Pair with my seafood sauce or a good squeeze of Kewpie mayo. It's time for a popcorn party!

1 or 2 uncooked crayfish tails (if more, double the batter and water)

500ml of rice bran oil (or other high smoke-point oil)

125g tempura flour

pinch of salt and pepper

180ml of ice-cold water

$\frac{1}{2}$ cup plain flour, for dusting

seafood sauce (page 216)

Prepare a batch of seafood sauce.

After removing the crayfish meat from the shell (see page 158), dice it into 2cm (1in) pieces. *There are natural crevices in the flesh, and I like to cut along these.*

Heat the oil in a wok or deep pan.

Meanwhile, in a mixing bowl, add the tempura flour and season with salt and pepper, then add the ice water and begin whisking. I also pop a few ice cubes in to stop the gluten from acting.

Check the oil is around 180 to 190°C (350 to 375°F). *Test with a drop of batter; if it floats, the temperature is right.*

Dust the crayfish lightly in flour before coating them in the tempura batter. Drop each piece in the oil slowly, 2 or 3 at a time. *I cook them in small batches to prevent them from sticking to each other, and so the oil doesn't cool down too quickly and slow the cooking.* Place the cooked pieces on a paper towel as you go.

Serve with a crunchy salad and seafood sauce.

LOBSTER ROLL

I almost feel like the lobster roll is fading out of fashion as quickly as the prawn cocktail – both of which I love, might I add. These days, lobster rolls are hard to come by unless you are lucky enough to make a trip to Bicheno, Tasmania, where the Lobster Shack makes Australia's best! I love a plateless vessel to eat from, and a roll overflowing with delicious crayfish definitely meets this criteria.

a bunch of chives, finely chopped

1 cup of Kewpie mayonnaise

juice of 1 lemon

salt and pepper

200g of unsalted butter

2 garlic cloves

a bunch of flat-leaf parsley, chopped

1 crayfish, halved

4 brioche hot dog rolls

Prepare a bed of coals away from your main fire and place a grate above it so you can cook over medium-high heat – *hot enough that you can only hold your hand 10cm above the cooking surface for 3 to 5 seconds.*

Finely chop chives and mix them in a bowl with Kewpie, a squeeze of lemon and a pinch of salt and pepper. Set aside.

Add the butter to the skillet and grate the garlic directly into the pan, then roughly toss in the parsley. Allow it all to melt together. Once it's melted, place crayfish on the grate, shells down, and spoon the butter mixture over the crayfish.

Cover it with a metal bowl, tray, camp oven or foil, and baste the cray meat every few minutes with the butter to coat well. Cook it it for 8 minutes or until the flesh is white and firm. Once cooked, remove the crayfish from the heat and set it aside.

Cut the buns before placing the cut sides into the leftover garlic butter, coating them well. Toast the buns for 2 minutes until golden and warm.

Add the crayfish to each bun and top with the mayo mixture.

FIRE PRAWN RISOTTO

There's so much I love about Australia and its incredible produce, but the good old prawn would be near the top of that list. Risotto has always been a dish I've really admired. If I'm ever out for dinner and it pops up on the menu, I'm pretty much ordering it every time. Arborio rice and prawns are fantastic friends, even if it takes a bit of patience to get it right. But trust me, the code is cracked once you do, and the risotto gates are open. So here's one for camping on a crisp night. Or in the middle of summer. You choose.

100g of unsalted butter

1 teaspoon of olive oil

1 shallot, diced

2 garlic cloves, diced

1 teaspoon of lemon zest

2 cups Arborio rice

1 cup of dry white wine

1 litre of fish stock

10 green prawns, peeled and deveined

juice of 1 lemon

¾ cup of grated parmigiano reggiano

freshly cracked black pepper

1 tablespoon of fresh tarragon leaves

Prepare a bed of coals away from your main fire and place a grate above it so you can cook in a camp oven over medium heat – *hot enough that you can only hold your hand 10cm above the cooking surface for 6 to 8 seconds.*

Melt half of the butter with all the olive oil in the camp oven. Add the diced shallot, garlic and lemon zest and sauté until they've softened. Pour in the Arborio rice and, using a wooden spoon, gently move the rice around the camp oven for about 3 minutes to cover it in the butter and oil. *Try not to overwork the rice, as this breaks up the starch.*

Remove some coals and reduce the heat to medium (*6 to 8 second hand hold*). Pour in the white wine and allow the liquid to reduce until it's sticky. Meanwhile, have the stock close by and add enough to cover the rice each time the liquid reduces to the sticky consistency. Continue until you've used all the stock. It should take around 15 to 20 minutes with gentle stirring.

Once you've added the final pour of stock, drop in the prawns and lemon juice and cook for 6 to 8 minutes or until the prawns are pink.

Add the remaining butter and grate in parmigiano reggiano. To gloss the rice, use care and make waves in the risotto by tossing it over itself, melting the butter and parmesan through without stirring or breaking the rice.

Serve with freshly cracked black pepper and fresh tarragon.

The trick to a perfect risotto is medium heat and plenty of patience, so get comfy with a glass of wine. It's better if you can heat the stock, but not essential. You can also swap the fish stock for vegetable.

I don't think there are too many times I won't leave a bowl of risotto aside purely to make arancini balls the next day.

PREP: 20 MIN   COOK: 45 MIN   SERVES: 4

PAELLA

Paella is the almighty king of all one-pot meals. It dates back centuries, first made by farm workers who'd cook it over a wood fire for lunch. It's the perfect camping meal and another fun and social one. Paella holds up well cooking directly over a flame, and I actually stoke the kindling under it to get that flame moving. Although you can cook it over gas, the smoky flavour you get into the rice from cooking it over a wood fire is unmatched, and after you've tasted it, it will be the only way you cook it in the future.

3 cups of chicken
stock

1 teaspoon of
crumbled saffron
threads

¼ cup of extra virgin
olive oil

1 large onion, finely
diced

2 garlic cloves,
crushed

1 red capsicum, diced

300g of chopped
tomatoes, roughly
2 large truss

2 tablespoons of
smoked paprika

2 tablespoons of salt

¼ cup of white wine

1 squid tube, sliced

1 ½ cups of bomba
rice

8 green prawns
whole shell on

8 large mussels in
shells, de-bearded
and scrubbed

½ cup of frozen peas

2 lemons

1 tablespoon of
chopped fresh
parsley

Prepare a small fire. You want it burning for at least 15 to 20 minutes to get a nice base. Meanwhile, prepare some small kindling to use for flame and heat control.

Place a grate on top of the fire, roughly 10 or so inches high, and at the edge of the grate, set a saucepan or billy to slowly heat the stock and saffron. *It's far better to have a nice warm stock if possible, but you can just pour the cold stock into the paella pan when it's time.*

Over a medium flame in a paella or large wide pan (*if you don't have a wide pan, use a large camp oven*), it's time to make a sofrito.
Add olive oil and sauté the onion, garlic, and red pepper. Cook for 4 to 5 minutes or until the onion is translucent, then add tomatoes, paprika, salt and white wine. *If you're not using warmed stock, add the saffron now.* Cook for 8 to 10 minutes or until the tomatoes are soft.

Add the squid, followed by the of stock and stir it all through.

It's time for the rice. Pour it into the pan so it makes a large cross, then, with a wooden spoon, evenly push out rice towards the sides. Give the pan a jiggle to set the rice evenly and resist all urges to do any more stirring.

Leave the pan to a vigorous simmer. Move coals or add kindling below to make it happen. Crack a beer or pour a red wine and enjoy the fragrance. After 10 to 12 minutes, add in prawns, mussels, and peas and gently push them into the rice so they're submerged as best as possible. No stirring!

Gently simmer for another 15 to 20 minutes. You may need to push some of the fire away to achieve this. *The time may vary depending on multiple factors, but don't worry if it takes longer. The dish is done when the prawns are pink, mussels open and liquid is absorbed.*

Listen to your rice for when the sound changes from a gurgle to a hiss. The rice has dried, and when it starts making a crackling sound and smells toasted, voila! Hopefully, you'll have a nice socarrat, a deliciously caramelised crust of golden rice that forms at the base. In my opinion, it's the best part of the paella. The trick is adding the right amount of stock for the rice to absorb, but not too much to harden without stirring.

When the rice is cooked, remove it from the heat and cover it with a tea towel for at least 5 minutes to give the dish time to settle and absorb the flavours. Serve with fresh lemon chunks and enjoy with my sangria from page 262.

Bomba is a Spanish short-grain rice that soaks in flavours incredibly well. It's the number one pick for paella, but if you can't find it, you can swap it for Arborio, no problems.

SHUCKING OYSTERS

Oysters are something that makes me extremely happy. I adore the fresh, crisp and salty flavour that they offer. For my husband, Lockie, oysters are life. They are his favourite food, and he often says if he only had one day left, it would be oysters on the menu. There's nothing better than a nice fresh oyster, and whether you're collecting them off the rocks or picking up a bag on the side of the road, I highly recommend shucking them yourself. It's a simple process, and the quality and freshness you get is unmatched. Pre-opened oysters should typically be consumed on the day of purchase, whereas un-shucked oysters can be stored in a bowl or airtight container with a damp tea towel over them in the fridge for up to seven days.

Here is the simple method I use to shuck oysters. You can use a tea towel and bench, but I prefer a shucking glove and oyster knife. Always be careful to protect your hand; oyster shells and the knife tip can give a nasty cut.

After scrubbing any mud or dirt from the shell, hold the oyster with the flat shell up and hinge toward you. Insert the knife tip into the hinge at around 15 degrees to the bottom shell and then twist it to break the hinge between the shells. You will typically hear a pop.

Slide the knife along the shell to separate the adductor muscle and release the top shell. The muscle is around the three o'clock position.

Turn the oyster around 180° and then insert a knife to separate the bottom part of the adductor muscle and release the oyster from the shell.

For presentation, insert a knife under the meat and gently roll it over. I'll do it if shucking oysters to serve them fresh, but I will generally skip this last step if I cook my Fire Oysters from (page 180).

FIRE OYSTERS

I first tried an oyster at Dad's restaurant in Hawkes Bay. I was nine, and he was confident I would like them Kilpatrick, given that they had bacon and sauce. As a child, I was a fussy eater and probably a nightmare for my chef father, but the obsession began when I ate that first oyster. Travelling in our Kombi, we never had an oven or a grill, but as we all love Kilpatrick, I decided to give them a go on the fire. They are better this way than I ever imagined, as the coals give the oyster and bacon a beautiful smoky flavour.

150g of streaky bacon

4 tablespoons of hickory barbecue sauce

2 tablespoons of Worcestershire

1 dozen oysters, shucked on the half shell

Tabasco (optional)

Prepare a bed of coals away from your main fire and place a grate above it so you can cook over medium-high heat – *hot enough that you can only hold your hand 10cm above the cooking surface for 3 to 5 seconds.*

Lay the rashers of bacon directly on the grate and cook until crispy, then remove and dice.

Mix the barbecue and Worcestershire sauce in a cup or bowl, spoon 1 teaspoon of sauce per oyster, and then top with 1 teaspoon of bacon. *I like adding a few drops of Tabasco to each oyster to really fire them up.*

Place oysters directly on the coals. Cook them for 3 to 5 minutes, then carefully remove them from the coals with tongs.

The oysters will be extremely hot – allow them to cool for a few minutes before diving in. Also, use caution not to leave oysters on coals for too long, as they can explode.

OYSTER MIGNONETTE

Now, I'm not going to lie to you, I don't know if there's a better way to enjoy a freshly shucked oyster than with a squeeze of lemon and a dash of Tabasco, but sometimes, something a little different has its place. I love gin, it's my go-to drink, and it also happens to pair beautifully with oysters.

Recently, when down in Coffin Bay, I played around with the famous Coffin Bay Spirits Rare Coastal Gin and a few easy ingredients to create a lovely afternoon mignonette. This one is perfect with an ice-cold gin and tonic.

1 tablespoon of peeled, seeded, and finely diced cucumber

1 tablespoon of finely diced shallots

3 tablespoons of distilled gin

2 tablespoons of red wine vinegar

1 teaspoon of sugar

1 dozen oysters, shucked on the half shell

Combine the cucumber and shallots in a mixing dish with the gin. Measure and dissolve sugar into red wine vinegar and add that as well.

Lay the oysters on a platter and spoon the mignonette on each. Serve with a cheeky gin and tonic.

Choose a gin with hints of juniper and citrus zest, as these flavours will make these oysters magical.

STICKY CHILLI & GINGER MUD CRAB

When we hit Broome, we got Broomed! Planning on staying just one week, we left over a month later. But that meant we could explore the beautiful Dampier Peninsula with good friends. In Lombadina, a little Aboriginal community with a small campground, the Bardi people welcomed us, and the boys became friends with a local, Bud. He took them mud-crabbing and came back to camp with enough for dinner. We pulled everything out of our pantries to see what we could make up and then stopped past the community bakery for a loaf of wood-fired bread. On the beach, we cooked up this recipe and ate it straight out of the camp oven while the sun went down. This recipe is now my favourite way to eat mud crab – the sticky, sweet chilli sauce pairs so beautifully with the crab meat.

4 garlic cloves

2 teaspoons of sea
  salt

6 lemongrass stalks

3 thumbs of ginger,
  roughly chopped

1 kaffir lime leaf,

4 large red chillies,
  save 1 for garnish

2 - 3 mud crabs,
  cleaned and de-
  gilled

50g of unsalted
  butter

1 cup of lime juice

½ cup of brown sugar

1 - 2 cups of water

flat-leaf parsley leaves

coriander leaves

Prepare a bed of coals away from your main fire and place a grate above it so you can cook in a camp oven over medium-high heat – *hot enough that you can only hold your hand 10cm above the cooking surface for 3 to 5 seconds.*

In a mortar and pestle, mash the garlic with salt to make a paste, then add the lemongrass and ginger, evenly muddling them down into the garlic. Finely chop the kaffir lime leaf and 3 of the chillies and add them to the mix and continue to muddle. *You can use a blender for a quicker, finer sauce.* Add the lime juice and brown sugar and give it a quick mix.

Break the mud crabs in half and crack open legs and claws with the back of a knife in multiple spots to maximise the crevices for the sauce to soak into the meat.

Add butter to the camp oven to melt before adding in the lemongrass mixture and cook until it's bubbling, then add a cup of water. You may need to add extra water if you have crabs above 1.5 to 2kg. *You don't need to cover them in liquid, but you need enough to spread the sauce around.*

Add in the crabs and stir and coat them with the sauce. It takes some hands to move the crab around the camp oven. Ensure the larger claws are at the bottom and the smaller legs are at the top. Place the lid on and cook for 7 to 10 minutes or until the crab is bright orange.

Serve with a sprinkle of parsley, coriander leaves, sliced red chilli and nice crusty bread with mates on a beach at sunset.

Use leftovers for crab cakes, which are delicious and can go a long way, mixed with leftover herbs and breadcrumbs.

CREAMY BACON & LEEK MUSSELS

I love a good pot of mussels and some crusty bread lathered with butter. It's all about the sauce and how amazing it is to dip your bread in after you've slurped a few mussels. This sauce is one that I've played with for a while and pairs so perfectly with a big pot of mussels. Now, I'm not going to lie. I'm very partial to green lips, which I grew up with, but I also love blue or black mussels. This recipe is perfect for all and will let any of them shine.

1.5kg of mussels in shells, de-bearded and well-scrubbed

1 tablespoon of butter

1 tablespoon of olive oil

200g of diced bacon

2 shallots, finely diced

1 medium leek, cut into moons

2 garlic cloves, finely chopped

$\frac{1}{2}$ cup of dry white wine

1 cup of cream

1 tablespoon of fish sauce

a pinch of finely chopped flat-leaf parsley

salt and freshly ground black pepper

a crusty French stick or my focaccia (page 226)

Prepare a bed of coals away from your main fire and place a grate above it so you can cook in a camp oven or skillet over medium heat – *hot enough that you can only hold your hand 10cm above the cooking surface for 6 to 8 seconds.*

Clean the mussels thoroughly under cold, running water and remove the beards. Discard any that have cracks or are open.

Add butter, olive oil, bacon, shallots, leek, and garlic to the camp oven and cook for about 4 minutes.

Add the mussels, followed by the wine, and let it steam with a lid on for 8 minutes. You will know they're cooked when all of the shells are open. Remove and discard any that are still closed. Leaving the sauce, remove the mussels with tongs and place them in serving bowls.

Stir in the cream, fish sauce and chopped parsley until the sauce is thickened (about 4 minutes), then season well with salt and pepper. Remove the sauce from the heat and spoon the sauce over the mussels, paying attention to the openings of the mussels.

Serve with buttery French stick or my camp oven focaccia.

Full-fat cream works best. Avoid using milk as it doesn't thicken correctly. Use any leftovers like my Mum, who makes wicked mussel fritters. Finely chop leftover mussel meat and mix it into a flour batter. Serve with dill yoghurt.

CHAPTER 5

SIDES
& SALADS

Here are some easy and quick accompaniments to many of my dishes throughout the book. I also love making many of these salads the night before a long drive, so we have a healthy and quick option for lunch.

RAW BROCCOLI SALAD

You will fall head over heels for this crunchy, moreish salad that's even full of greens. I love to take it to a camp party as it cuts so well with meat. It's quick to prepare, and you'll be returning for more mouthfuls.

200g of bacon, diced

1 - 2 heads of broccoli

1 red onion, diced

2 cups of mild cheese, grated

1 cup of Kewpie mayonnaise

juice of 1 lemon

2 cloves of garlic, grated

extra virgin olive oil

salt and pepper

Pop the bacon straight into a skillet and cook it for approximately 5 minutes until it's crispy and golden. Scoop it out of the pan onto scrunched-up paper towel to cool.

Meanwhile, wash and dry the broccoli, then roughly chop it, including the stems. Pop it in a large bowl with the red onion and grated cheese.

Prepare the dressing in a separate bowl by grating the garlic into the Kewpie mayonnaise and lemon juice, then give it a mix.

Toss the dressing over the broccoli and stir it through. I like to add the bacon on top last. Add a drizzle of olive oil with a sprinkle of salt and pepper to finish.

ZUCCHINI RIBBON SALAD

SERVES: 4

COOK: 10 MIN

PREP: 5 MIN

Zucchinis are my favourite vegetable. As a 20-year-old dying to have green thumbs, zucchini was the first successful veggie from my garden. I've used them in so many recipes and never got sick of them. This recipe will never grow old and will always excite me to eat. It is zingy, crunchy, spicy and salty, which is why it works so well with grilled fish.

3 zucchinis, peeled into ribbons

juice and zest of 2 lemons

salt and pepper

1 red chilli

a bunch of fresh mint

100g of soft feta

extra virgin olive oil

Shave ribbons of zucchini using a peeler or mandolin. *Save the centre for green juice, or chop and freeze it to add to bolognaise.* Lay the ribbons evenly on a plate and cover them generously with lemon juice. Add salt and pepper to season.

Deseed a large red chilli for a mild salad, or thinly sliced chilli rounds with seeds if, like me, you love a good kick. Pick and wash mint leaves before drying them with a paper towel. Slap the leaves between your palms to release the flavours and tear them over the salad.

Crumble feta over the top with the zest of lemon and a glug of olive oil.

CHARRED CAESAR

Anytime I'm invited to a barbecue, I like to take a Caesar salad. It's a great all-rounder and so easy to put together. Charring lettuce is a great spin on this timeless classic. It is both warming and has smoky tones, with a buttery finish that is showstopping for your next barbecue.

200g of bacon

4 medium cos lettuce hearts, quartered

1 cup of day-old sourdough slices

3 anchovies

4 whole hard-boiled eggs

1 cup of parmesan cheese

2 tablespoons of olive oil

CREAMY DRESSING

3 anchovies

$\frac{1}{2}$ cup of freshly grated parmesan

$\frac{1}{2}$ cup of Kewpie mayonnaise

1 $\frac{1}{2}$ tablespoons of extra virgin olive oil

2 cloves of garlic, grated

1 tablespoon of lemon juice

1 teaspoon of Worcestershire

1 teaspoon of wholegrain mustard

Prepare a bed of coals away from your main fire and place a grate above it so you can cook over high heat – *hot enough that you can only hold your hand 10cm above the cooking surface for 2 to 4 seconds.*

For the dressing, mash 3 anchovies with a fork to break them up. Grate the parmesan into a bowl and mix the mayo and olive oil into the cheese using a whisk or fork. Add in the garlic and mashed anchovies.

Spoon in the lemon juice, Worcestershire sauce, and mustard and give it a good mix, then refrigerate until ready to use.
Fry the bacon in a skillet until it's crispy.
At the same time, quarter the cos lettuce into wedges and brush each with olive oil. Place the wedges on the grate, cut sides down, and press them down to sear for 2 to 3 minutes. Remove the lettuce and bacon from the heat and set them aside, but toast the sourdough in the bacon residue until golden.

On a serving dish, assemble the salad, starting with the sourdough slices, then the lettuce, bacon, and anchovies. Set the eggs on the side and drizzle the dressing over the tip. Generously grate parmesan over the top and finish with a drizzle of olive oil.

Grilled chicken skewers are a perfect accompaniment to this salad.

SWEET POTATO SALAD

After-school chores always included peeling a pot of potatoes, usually a mix of kumara and Desiree, which were grown in Grandma's garden. They were served on rotation between mashed, roasted and boiled with butter. I'm not complaining; they are yummy those ways, but on a beautiful summer day, sweet potatoes are perfect with feta and rocket. This salad is excellent with lamb or pork.

2 cups of pearl couscous

1 ½ cups of chicken stock or water

zest and juice of one lemon

2 large sweet potatoes, diced with the skin on

extra virgin olive oil

salt and pepper

200g of rocket

½ cup of slithered almonds

100g of Danish feta, crumbled

Toast the couscous in a skillet over medium-high heat for 8 minutes, tossing frequently until golden. Add in the stock or water, letting it cook for 15 minutes more. Grate in the lemon zest and allow it to stand and cool.

Meanwhile, massage the sweet potato in olive oil, salt, and pepper and fry it in a pan over medium heat for 15 minutes, tossing them frequently.

Toss the rocket, fried sweet potatoes, almonds, and crumbled feta into the cooled couscous. Finish it with salt, pepper and lemon juice.

MISO CHARRED
BOK CHOY

The easiest and simplest accompaniment to many of my dishes. It's vibrantly green and full of umami.

2 tablespoons of miso paste

1 tablespoon of soy sauce

1 tablespoon of grated ginger

1 tablespoon of sesame oil

1 tablespoon of mirin

3 medium bok choy

Prepare a bed of coals away from your main fire and place a grate above it so you can cook over medium-high heat – *hot enough that you can only hold your hand 10cm above the cooking surface for 3 to 5 seconds.*

Mix the miso paste, soy sauce, grated ginger, sesame oil and mirin in a bowl.

Cut the cleaned bok choy down the centre to halve, and smear the miso mixture over the cut side.

Place the bok choy, cut side down, and sear and create a crust. Remove and serve immediately.

LEMON COUSCOUS

This side is perfect for my chicken tagine from page 132.

1 cup of chicken stock

½ cup of water

1 cup of couscous

20g of unsalted
   butter

the juice and zest of
   1 lemon

1 teaspoon of extra-
   virgin olive oil

To make an easy camp couscous, simply boil chicken stock and water. Once bubbling, remove it from the heat, add the couscous with a knob of butter, and allow it to stand for 10 minutes.

Fluff the couscous with a fork, add the zest and season with lemon juice and a drizzle of olive oil. Serve with giant spoons of Moroccan chicken.

DUKKAH CARROT

We've all had dukkah on bread. It's a balanced mix of nuts, seeds and spices, great for crusting chicken or fish, dipping with olive oil, or adding over the top of roasted carrots. I have always been a big fan of dukkah — the warm flavours are just perfect.

2 tablespoons of honey

1 tablespoon of olive oil

3 tablespoons of dukkah

8 - 12 assorted carrots

2 tablespoons of unsalted butter

100g of feta

In a large bowl, mix the honey, olive oil and dukkah.

Wash the carrots and halve them lengthways, then toss them into the mixture, coating well.

Heat the butter in a skillet or roasting pan over medium heat. Place the carrots evenly flat-side-down and cover with a lid or foil and cook for 15 to 20 minutes before turning. Cook for another 10 to 15 minutes, watching closely and shuffling the pan from time to time.

Serve with crumbled feta a drizzle of the remaining honey liquid over the top.

Pair these carrots with labneh (page 203) and your favourite protein.

JAPANESE CABBAGE SALAD

A highlight of my time in Japan is this simple salad, the hero ingredient being cabbage. It is hard to believe cabbage could taste so good, it is ever so simple, yet addictive – I am certain you will love it.

PREP: 5 MIN

COOK: 10 MIN

SERVES: 2-4

$\frac{1}{2}$ cup of sesame seeds

1 teaspoon of soy sauce

1 teaspoon of rice wine vinegar

1 teaspoon of mirin

1 teaspoon of sesame oil

2 tablespoons of Kewpie mayonnaise

$\frac{1}{2}$ a white cabbage, finely sliced

Toast the sesame seeds in a hot pan until they start to turn golden. Remove them from the heat and whiz them in a blender until smooth. Mix in the soy sauce, rice wine vinegar, mirin, sesame oil and mayonnaise. Combine the sesame mixture with the mayonnaise.

Toss the cabbage and sesame dressing together. It's perfect with my yakitori sticks for a Japanese-inspired dinner.

This dressing is so flavourful and great on pasta or raw broccoli.

LABNEH

Decorate it, dip it or use it to escalate your meals – labneh is the easiest and simplest homemade cheese that graces our table most weeks. It always accompanies Moroccan lamb.

3 cups of high-quality Greek yoghurt

1 tablespoon of sea salt

cheesecloth

Mix the salt into the yoghurt.

Spoon the yoghurt into the centre of a cheesecloth, leaving enough room to tie the edges over a wooden spoon.

Suspend the yoghurt cheesecloth over a bowl with the wooden spoon ends resting high enough to allow the excess liquid to drip while it's left for 24 hours.

Great with lamb, fish or as a chilli dip.

AUTUMN PUMPKINS

PREP: 5 MIN   COOK: 1 HOUR   SERVES: 2-4

The colours of autumn and the smell of a roasting pumpkin are two reasons I love farmers' markets as the weather cools. I often make a beeline for a fresh veggie stand, looking for fresh garlic and butternut pumpkin. If I find them, this is what we eat.

1 medium butternut pumpkin

1 tablespoon of sumac

1 tablespoon of paprika

1 tablespoon of sesame seeds

2 tablespoons of agave syrup or honey

2 - 3 tablespoons of olive oil

MINT AND YOGHURT DRESSING

1 clove of garlic, grated

1 tablespoon of roughly chopped mint

1 cup of natural Greek yoghurt

1 tablespoon of lemon juice

1 teaspoon of honey

salt and pepper, to taste

Cut the pumpkin lengthways, peel it and hollow out the seeds. Place the pumpkin flat on a foil- and baking paper-lined skillet. Make cuts in the top like the rungs of a ladder, but not all the way through. *Sometimes we make the cuts after the first cook as it's a bit easier with the knife.*

Combine the spices in a small bowl with the agave and olive oil, and brush it over the pumpkin.

Cover and place on a bed of coals at medium heat – *hot enough that you can only hold your hand 10cm above them for about 5 to 8 seconds.*

After 15 to 20 minutes, remove the pumpkin from the coals and give it a second brush of the mixture. Return it to the coals for 30 to 40 minutes, or until soft.

Meanwhile, prepare the mint and yoghurt dressing. Combine the garlic, mint and yoghurt. Whisk in the lemon juice and honey with a fork, then season with salt and pepper.

When the pumpkin is ready, serve with dollops of yoghurt on top.

SLAW, TWO WAYS

We use this slaw a lot. With pineapple, it's perfect with pulled pork tacos. Without pineapple, it's great with brisket.

½ a red cabbage

1 red onion

1 cup of diced, fresh pineapple, optional

1 cup of fresh shredded coriander

½ cup of Kewpie mayonnaise

1 tablespoon of apple cider vinegar

2 teaspoons of honey

salt and freshly ground pepper

Shred the cabbage and onion with a sharp knife (or a potato peeler is a perfect tool for this). Mix in the diced pineapple and coriander.

Combine the kewpie, apple cider vinegar and honey in a bowl, and toss it through the slaw. Season well. It's best if it gets to rest for an hour before serving.

SMOKER MAC CHEESE

We love this really simple macaroni cheese with brisket, and it's easy to make on your barbeque or smoker.

2 cups of macaroni

50g of unsalted butter

2 tablespoons of plain flour

1 cup of milk

2 cups of grated cheese

salt and pepper

½ cup wholemeal breadcrumbs

½ cup grated gruyere

Bring a saucepan of salty water to a boil, add the pasta and cook until al dente. Strain and set it aside.

Meanwhile, melt butter in a saucepan and spoon in the flour. Once little bubbles appear, add milk, and stir vigorously until it's thick and smooth. Sprinkle a handful of grated cheese bit by bit and stir as it melts.

Pour it over the macaroni, season with salt and pepper and spread it evenly into a 26cm (10in) baking dish.

Rub the breadcrumbs with grated gruyere in a bowl and arrange it into clumps over the pasta.

Bake in a barbecue or smoker for 20 minutes until the top is golden and crunchy.

CHAPTER 6

SAUCES
& DIPS

I am a serious condiment lover and have been known to douse my hot chips in seafood sauce; I know it's a little weird, but don't mock it 'til you try it. Here are a few sauces that I always make and then keep bottled in the fridge. I have also included a few dips that we all enjoy and a famous Kiwi one that is super easy and very addictive.

SPICY RED PLUM SAUCE

Dad's spicy plum sauce is a fond memory, peppery and sweet. This pairs so well with meats, especially when they're smoked.

1 lemon,

2.5kg of red plums

5 $\frac{1}{2}$ cups of malt vinegar

4 cups of brown sugar

8 garlic cloves

4 teaspoons of ground pepper

2 teaspoons of ground allspice

1 teaspoon of ground cloves

1 star anise

$\frac{1}{2}$ teaspoon of cayenne pepper

2 tablespoons of salt

Using a potato peeler, peel 2 slithers of the lemon peel from top to bottom, avoiding the pith as much as possible. Juice the lemon. Add all the ingredients to a deep pot and bring it to the boil. Let it simmer for 8 minutes. I like to use a slotted spoon to stir and move the plums, to separate the flesh from the seed and skin.

Once it's foaming, remove it from the heat and sieve out the pulpy bits, skins, and stones. Place back on the heat and bring it back to a boil for 4 to 5 minutes to make a syrupy sauce.

Remove it from the heat and let it cool for immediate use.

This makes a lot, so it's perfect for bottling.

MUSHROOM
SAUCE

Everyone loves a good creamy mushroom sauce and this one will go perfectly on my steak sandwich, a steak or a good old chicken snitty.

60g of unsalted butter

½ a tablespoon of olive oil

2 garlic cloves

1 shallot, finely diced

300g of assorted mushrooms, finely sliced

½ a cup of chicken or vegetable broth

1 cup of cream

pinch of salt and pepper

2 teaspoons of fresh thyme leaves

Heat a skillet to medium heat. Drop in the butter and olive oil with the garlic and shallots. *I am a fan of solo garlic (also known as elephant garlic) for this recipe. It adds a subtle flavour to the sauce.*

Slowly allow the mushrooms to soften and absorb all the butter before adding the broth. Let the broth steam off before the cream goes in. Swirl and see the mushroom colour appear throughout the sauce, then season with salt and pepper to your liking.

Pluck the thyme leaves from the stems to sprinkle into the sauce. Best used immediately.

HUMMUS

Hummus is delicious. We make a batch of it weekley and have it with flat bread and vegetables. Alba loves it so much she eats it by the spoonful.

350g jar of chickpeas

1 - 2 cloves of garlic

2 tablespoons of tahini

$\frac{1}{4}$ tablespoon of lemon juice

salt to taste

$\frac{1}{2}$ cup of iced water

1 tablespoon of extra virgin olive oil

Strain the chickpeas and keep a quarter of the liquid. *I put the juice in the fridge to keep it as cold as possible.* Blend the garlic and chickpeas, making a thick paste. Pour in the tahini, lemon juice, and salt and continue to blend.

Lastly, blend in the ice water and chickpea juice (aquafaba), followed by the olive oil.

Top with dukkah or sumac spice.

You can make this with a mortar and pestle. Use an ice cube to keep the mixture cool while thumping the chickpeas.

TZATZIKI

Tzatziki has to be the easiest, most delicious dip I know. This recipe is inspired by a mezze plate we enjoyed at the seaside, one Grecian summer ago. It is creamy, zingy and smooth. Once you make it, I'm certain you will dollop it on almost everything.

1 cucumber

1 cup of natural Greek yoghurt

2 tablespoons of lemon juice

½ tablespoon of extra virgin olive oil

1 garlic clove, grated

pinch of salt

1 tablespoon of chopped mint (optional)

Finely grate a cucumber and squeeze out the excess water in a tea towel. Do more grating if you don't quite have half a cup's worth.

Combine the cucumber, yoghurt, lemon juice, olive oil, garlic, salt, and mint in a mixing bowl.

Serve with pitas or lamb.

Full-fat Greek yoghurt is best, and far creamier for a good outcome.

SEAFOOD SAUCE

DILL SAUCE

I love this on hot chips, but of course, it's best with prawns in a 1970s-style prawn cocktail.

A quick, summery sauce to enjoy with fish, especially salmon.

1 part Kewpie mayonnaise

1 part tomato sauce

1 part Worcestershire sauce

½ part Tabasco (optional)

Combine all the ingredients and enjoy. It'll keep in a jar for up to 3 weeks refrigerated.

You might have noticed my chilli fever. I'm not sure why or when it started, but I'm hooked, and I like things hot.

1 cup of sour cream

1 teaspoon of Dijon mustard

1 tablespoon of finely chopped fresh dill

1 tablespoon of roughly chopped brine capers

the juice of 1 lemon

sea salt and black pepper

extra virgin olive oil

Combine the sour cream, mustard, dill, capers, lemon juice, a good pinch of sea salt and some cracked black pepper in a mixing bowl. If you use salt flakes here, the texture of the large crystals will serve as a lovely counterpart to the sauce's creaminess. Stir well to combine and return to the fridge to chill.

MISO DIP

KIWI ONION DIP

Fresh vegetables served with this yummy dip has to be the perfect beachside snack.

In New Zealand, you won't go to the rugby, a party or barbecue without taking this dip or finding it on the table.

3 tablespoons of white miso paste

⅓ cup of Kewpie mayonnaise

1 garlic clove, grated

1 - 2 tablespoons of honey

2 tablespoons of rice wine vinegar

1 teaspoon of toasted sesame seeds

Combine all the ingredients and let it chill in the fridge for an hour.

If you don't have an hour, you can serve this straight away.

If you don't have Kewpie, use Greek yoghurt.

230ml of Nestle reduced fat cream

a packet of French onion soup mix

the juice of 1 lemon

sea salt potato chips

Pour the reduced fat cream and French onion soup into a large mixing bowl. Mix until well combined.

Squeeze in lemon juice and give it a mix before setting it in the fridge for at least 30 minutes.

Serve with sea salt potato chips.

CHIMICHURRI

I've played around with this recipe for a while, adding different ingredients and seeing how they work. In the end, I came to the conclusion that nothing compares to the age-old traditional style. As the saying goes, "Why change a good thing?". Below is the best chimichurri, but it's versatile enough to be modified to your liking. I like mine super-hot, but hey, that's just me.

4 - 5 garlic cloves

2 level teaspoons of flaky salt

1 cup of finely chopped parsley

5 teaspoons of fresh oregano or 1 $\frac{1}{2}$ teaspoons of dried

2 small red chillies — deseeded or seeded to your liking

1 cup of olive oil

4 tablespoons of red wine vinegar

1 teaspoon freshly cracked pepper

Place the garlic into the mortar with the flaky salt and begin pounding until broken, then add the parsley and oregano and keep mashing.

Finely chop the chilli and add it in, giving it all a heavy mix. Pour in the olive oil and red wine vinegar.

Season with pepper, give it a final stir and chill in the fridge for 30 to 40 minutes.

Use a mortar and pestle to make this authentically, as this ignites the herbs and intensifies the flavour. But it'll also works in a blender.

SOME LIKE
IT HOT

I, for one, am one of them. I like to add heat to nearly everything I eat. I have even been known to carry a sneaky bottle of Tabasco sauce in my handbag.

Chillies are a natural way to add flavour and fun to just about any meal. It's not just the endorphin release that has me hooked, but also the flavour profile different chillies offer. I use chilli in most of my cooking, even for meals I make for my children. Understanding where the heat comes from and how to moderate it enables you to use these beautiful fruits for their flavour and health benefits, even if you are not the biggest fan of hot food.

Chillies get their heat from a chemical called capsaicin, which is meant to deter mammals that want to eat the fruit. Eating capsaicin tricks our brain into activating pain receptors, and our body releases hormones, which give us an energy rush and boosts our sense of well-being. No wonder we love chillies!

Capsaicin resides in the white membrane where the seeds gather. The seeds contain very little heat, and only when they have been in contact with the membrane's oil do they become hot. Removing the membrane and seeds entirely will lessen the heat and let you enjoy the incredible flavour and benefits without running for a glass of milk!

I'm sure you have heard the saying that the smaller the chilli, the hotter it is, and a broader or longer chilli will be milder. It's a good guideline, but there can be some exceptions, so it's always best to taste a small piece first to ensure it won't overpower your whole dish.

Preparing a Chilli

• Cut off the stalk.

• Cut in half down the length of the chilli.

• Remove the membrane and seeds from each side with a teaspoon and discard. If you like it hot, leave the membrane and remove the seeds. Alternatively, if you like it extra mild, you can scrape out the innermost layer of flesh, removing even more capsaicin.

• Cut the two halves into fine strips lengthways, then across for a fine dice.

Although there is an enormous number of chillies out there, the ones over-page are what I cook with most often.

Habanero (extremely hot) – The flavour of a habanero is just out of this world. They are sweet, fruity, crunchy and pungent. It pairs perfectly with sweet foods and has a mild, smoky flavour that I like to enhance by blistering directly on coals, removing the skin and dicing before adding to a dish.

Birds Eye (very hot) – This little guy can pack a punch! Commonly found in Southeast Asian dishes, it is fruity and peppery with some serious kick. Fantastic paired with prawns, fish, soups, salads and curry pastes.

Cayenne (moderately hot to hot) – This chilli's heat falls right in the middle of jalapeño and bird's eye, offering a lovely, fruity flavour. I use it both whole and ground, and I'm sure most of you will have a jar of it in your spice cupboard. Cayenne pepper is great to add to just about any dish. I use it predominantly in curries, sauces and marinades.

Jalapeño (mild) – Jalapeño is a worldwide favourite, and rightfully so. It has just the right amount of heat without going overboard. Jalapeño is fantastic roasted or stuffed as poppers, and it's a lovely addition to a nice fresh salad. They pair perfectly with Mexican and Spanish cuisine, which often use it pickled. I will always have a jar and a few fresh ones with me, as this is the chilli I use the most. Jalapeño offers a versatile flavour profile, similar to green capsicum but with a kick. Dried and smoked jalapeños are called chipotle and are another favourite, with a long shelf life to have tucked away in your van cupboard.

CHAPTER 7

BREADS

I have always enjoyed making as much as I can from scratch, and all the more since living on the road. There is so much satisfaction in pulling a warm bread out of our camp oven. In this chapter, I share with you my quick and easy doughs, pasta, and flatbreads. They are fun to make, and this is a great way to get the kids involved in cooking.

CAMP OVEN FOCACCIA

Whenever my grandmother made her Saturday morning loaf, there was always a scramble to get the first hot slice. We would sit around the kitchen table, smearing jam and dunking it into our tea. It was what inspired me, while the world was learning to make sourdough bugs throughout 2020, to perfect focaccia in a camp oven. It is more forgiving than other breads, making it perfect for camping. It takes a night to rest and then a quick 20-minute cook.

420ml of lukewarm water

1 teaspoon of honey or sugar

1 tablespoon of olive oil, plus extra for rising

2 teaspoons or 8g of active yeast

1 teaspoon of salt

500g of oo flour

100g of cherry tomatoes or olives, halved

Whisk together the water, honey, olive oil, yeast, and salt in a measuring jug and leave it for five minutes until the yeast bubbles and foams.

Add the liquids to the flour in a large bowl and mix until combined, slightly kneading and scraping down the sides until you have a rough ball of dough. Drizzle olive oil over the top, ensuring it is well coated. Cover and place in the fridge for 10 minutes.

Oil your hands (so the dough doesn't stick) and stretch the dough by pulling it up and over itself. Repeat the stretch 3 times, turning the bowl 90° for each pull. Let it rest for 10 minutes and repeat the stretch and pull 2 more times. *Each time, the dough should seem much silkier and less sticky.* Cover and leave it in the fridge overnight.

Prepare a bed of coals away from your main fire and place a grate above it.

Fit a trivet to your camp oven and line the inside with oiled baking paper. With olive oil on your hands, gently stretch the dough to fit the shape of the oven and use your fingers to make dimples and bubbles. Dot cherry tomatoes or olives over the top, drizzle it with olive oil and sprinkle over some flaky sea salt.

Put the lid on the camp oven and set it over the heat. Move about 80 per cent of the coals to the lid and bake the bread for 20 to 25 minutes until it's golden brown.

Serve it in thick slices.

The trick to great bread is using scales to measure the ingredients accurately. Then rest, rest, rest! After pulling the bread from the oven, allow it to cool for 30 minutes. The beautiful pockets will rise, and the squish of the bread forms. Reheat it gently over the fire if you want to serve it warm.

FRY BREAD

Making fry bread transports me back to my family marae. The wharekai (dining room) was my place of calm as a child, and I loved sipping tea with fry bread in hand, watching how synchronised everyone was. Clouds of flour would puff into the air, and my aunties were always laughing aloud as they rolled the dough before dropping them in pots of oil. They puff right up and leave pockets inside for butter and golden syrup.

2 teaspoons or 8g of active yeast

1 tablespoon of honey

2 ½ cups of warm water

5 cups of all-purpose flour

a pinch of salt

1L of rice bran or other high smoke-point oil

golden syrup and butter, to serve

Dissolve the yeast and honey in the water and allow it to froth for 5 minutes.

Mix the flour and salt in a large bowl, then mix the wet ingredients into the dry. Scrape out the dough and lay it onto a floured bench. Fold the dough gently until it's combined into a rough ball.

Place the dough back into the bowl to rise in a warm place. Allow it to double in size over an hour.

Punch the dough, flip it onto a floured bench and begin rolling and cutting into golf ball-sized squares.

Heat a wok or deep pan of oil. You will know the temperature is right when you drop a small amount of dough in, and it floats to the top and bubbles. Carefully drop the dough squares in and fry in batches for 5 to 7 minutes, letting them puff and brown before rolling them over.

Drain on paper towels, and enjoy with golden syrup and butter.

This recipe is wonderful with a cinnamon sugar coating or even as a burger bun.

FLATBREAD

We have this bread all the time. It is really simple and versatile, and we often just cook straight on the coals.

500g of natural Greek yoghurt

500g of self-raising flour

pinch of salt and pepper

1 tablespoon of baking powder

1 teaspoon of oregano

8 tablespoons of extra virgin olive oil

Mix the yoghurt, flour, salt, baking powder, and oregano until thoroughly combined into a smooth ball, then let it rest for 30 minutes.

Cut it into 8 pieces on a floured surface and roll them out into ovals.

Heat a hot skillet to medium-high, and with a tablespoon of olive oil, fry each bit of dough until slightly charred on each side. Alternatively, brush oil on each and cook them straight in the coals.

These are perfect with Moroccan lamb, gyros or any other time you need flatbread.

CORNBREAD

What is brisket without cornbread? I love making cornbread for many other dishes as well. It's easy and was made for a skillet.

The trick here is to get a nice hot skillet. When the batter hits, it must sizzle. This is how you know you're about to achieve the perfect crust.

1 ¼ cups of cornflour

¾ cup of all-purpose flour

2 teaspoons of baking powder

½ teaspoon of baking soda

¼ cup of sugar

1 teaspoon of sea salt

1 ⅓ cups of milk

2 eggs

50g of unsalted butter, melted

Cut a sheet of baking paper to fit a 30cm cast iron skillet. Adjust the temperature on your smoker to around 204°C (400°F) and preheat it and the skillet for 15 minutes.

Sift the cornflour, flour, baking powder and baking soda into a mixing bowl, and add the sugar and salt. Whisk in the milk, eggs and melted butter.

Pour the batter into the preheated skillet and bake for 20 to 25 minutes. The cornbread is done when the top is firm and a bamboo or metal skewer comes out clean.

Remove it from the skillet carefully and allow the bread to cool, cut it into cake slices, and enjoy with your brisket plate.

CORN TORTILLAS

After making this and seeing how easy and rewarding it is, you will never buy store bought tortillas again. My little girl, Alba, loves helping with this one as it's lots of fun. After these tortillas are cooked, you can also cut them into triangles and fry them to make corn chips, another thing you probably won't buy again after tasting how delicious these turn out.

2 cups of masa harina

1 cup of warm tap water

2 tablespoons of water at room temperature (for damp hands)

Place the masa harina into a mixing bowl and add in the water. Mix thoroughly with your hands for 2 to 3 minutes until a tacky ball forms. If the ball is dry, add a little more water by wetting your hands as you knead.

Divide the dough into 12 golf ball-size balls, and cover with a damp cloth to keep them moist.

We carry a tortilla press which is a very useful little device. We use it for crushing garlic and nuts and making thin patties. If you don't have one, use the base of your camp oven – it works perfectly.

Place a sheet of baking paper on the bottom disc of the press (or bench). Add a ball of dough, cover it with another sheet of baking paper and press down firmly. Rotate the tortilla 90° and press again.

Peel off the paper and place the tortilla onto an ungreased, hot grate or skillet at medium heat for 30 seconds. Turn them over and cook for a further 45 seconds.

Place in a damp tea towel to keep warm until ready to serve.

Masa harina is available from specialty grocers or international food stores. I buy 1kg at a time and it lasts for so long in my caravan pantry, and I can always make tortillas, even in the middle of the outback.

HANDMADE PASTA

Making your own pasta is a no brainer and, in my opinion, far superior to bought pasta. It's fresh and enjoyable to make. Another fantastic recipe to get the little helpers involved.

300g of 00 flour

100g of 00 flour, for dusting

3 eggs

Place 300g of flour straight onto a clean bench and make a well in the centre.

Crack the eggs into the well and use a fork to break the yolks, and whisk slowly. Try to keep the walls of flour in place until the yolks and whites are completely incorporated.

Collapse the flour walls into the eggs using your hands. *By now, the egg and flour should be binding and look rough, like scone dough.*

Scrape any loose bits together and knead them into a ball. *It may seem crumbly, and it will take some work and warmth from your hands before you start to see a shiny dough.* Using your palm, push and stretch the ball. While doing so, use your other hand to turn the ball 90° – fold and repeat for around 10 to 15 minutes. The better the knead, the better the pasta, as the flour becomes more hydrated.

Once you are happy with your dough, wrap it tightly in beeswax or eco-cling wrap. Allow it to rest for 30 minutes to an hour at room temperature.

Unwrap the dough, place it in the centre of a dusted surface, and then cut it in half. Re-wrap 1 ball so it doesn't dry out and set it aside.

Use a rolling pin and roll the dough into an oval. Spin it 90° and roll it out to a circle. Fold the pasta onto itself like a book, then roll it out some more. Repeat 2 to 3 times, with plenty of flour dusting.

The final roll should be long and paper thin. Fold each side into the middle and then fold it again to look like a folded sheet. Cut it lengthways to the pasta thickness you desire. Shake and set it aside with a dusting of flour.

Store the pasta dough balls in the fridge for two days or freeze them for up to one month.

Repeat with the second ball.

Cook for 2 to 3 minutes in salted boiling water until al dente.

HANDMADE PIZZA DOUGH

Good dough is the foundation of a perfect pizza, and I'm not going to lie, there's definitely a science to getting it right. The dough below is for a Neapolitan-style pizza, so follow the steps to create a beautiful, light-yet-chewy, bubbly crust. This recipe is for four pizzas and relies on cold fermentation over 48 hours, so some planning is involved, but trust me, it's worth it.

780ml of lukewarm water

3g of active yeast

1200g of oo flour

36g of salt

Whisk the lukewarm water and active yeast in a bowl or large jug until bubbly. *I prefer active yeast that needs water to help it bloom. You can add instant yeast directly to the flour – both work.*

Mix the flour and salt in a separate bowl, then add the water and yeast. Using your hand as a paddle, move the flour into the centre of the bowl and start mixing until the flour is absorbed, elastic and a ball is formed.

Place the dough ball onto a flour-dusted surface and start kneading for at least 10 minutes; *I normally knead for 15 to 20 minutes or until the dough is stretchy and smooth.* Tuck the dough under itself as you rotate it, to create a ball.

Cover an oiled bowl with a damp tea towel, or eco-cling wrap and place it into the fridge for 24 hours. Remove it from the fridge and bring it to room temperature over an hour. Cut the dough into balls of 280g each. *It is best to use scales here.* Cover and put them back into the fridge for another 24 hours.

On pizza day, wrap the balls of dough you're not working on so they don't dry out. Stretch each to size by flipping and using your knuckles to pull the dough to the desired shape, size, and thickness. They should make a 14in pizza base.

Top, cook, enjoy.

I often double the recipe and freeze a few dough balls individually in Tupperware containers for next time. Defrost the dough in the fridge overnight and bring it to room temperature for an hour before cooking.

CHAPTER 8

SWEETS & PARTY STARTERS

These recipes are my love letters to home. Throughout this chapter, I share the heritage recipes I always cooked with my grandmother, Nanny. Most weekends, she and I pulled out big Tupperware containers of flour and sugar to make cakes, slices, and scones, ready for my school lunchbox and any visitors that would drop by. I love how this was such an everyday practice for our grandparents' generation. I now enjoy carrying on this tradition, and I always try to have homemade goods ready to share with neighbouring campers over a hot cuppa.

PREP: 5 MIN   COOK: 10 MIN   SERVES: 4

NANNY'S PAVLOVA

Nanny's pavlova is a cracker, and I call her whenever I make it so she can read me the recipe. I've cooked it a hundred times, so I know the recipe perfectly, but I just like hearing her read it to me. She is from the South Island and, despite being from a different world, fell in love with my handsome Māori grandfather. When he took her to his marae, there would be a lineup for this fluffy, chewy and creamy roll. This recipe has been handed down to me from her as a quick and easy microwave version that's similar to a roulade. So, this is for all you folk out there with a beautiful, big caravan and a microwave, or when you find one in a camp ktichen.

4 egg whites

$\frac{1}{2}$ cup of castor sugar

$\frac{1}{4}$ cup of desiccated
coconut

1 cup of fresh cream

1 fresh mango,
slithered

2 fresh passionfruit

Beat the egg whites and sugar to make fluffy stiff peaks. *When you can make a figure-8 in the whites, and it keeps its shape, that's perfect.* Set it aside for now.

Toast the coconut over high heat in a skillet until golden. *Move the coconut around with a wooden spoon to achieve an even colouring.* Once done, spread it onto a sheet of baking paper.

Lay more baking paper over the tray of your microwave and cut it to shape. Pour the egg whites straight on. Ensure it is level and cook it in the microwave for 4 minutes. *The mixture will puff up and look like marshmallow.*

While it's still hot, work quickly to flip the pav onto the toasted coconut. It's best to do it immediately so the coconut will stick. Leave it to cool.

Meanwhile, whip cream until it's thickened and smear it over the pav, but leave a border around the edges. Arrange the mango and passionfruit in the centre and, using your palm, lift and roll the pavlova from each side so the edges meet in the middle. Secure it with toothpicks and leave it to set in the freezer for at least 30 minutes (or in the fridge for longer).

Serve generous slices from the log.

Depending on the season, this is also great with strawberries, raspberries, blueberries or kiwifruit.

GOLDEN STEAM PUDDING

A gooey golden steamed pudding is to die for, and this is the dessert most often cooked in a hangi. I have discovered that this moreish, soft loaf also fares perfectly in a camp oven. This recipe was originally my auntie's, but here it's with my own twist. You'll need a couple of large tomato tins and some muslin wrap. Enjoy it with cream or ice cream. Who said desserts around a campfire had to be boring?

2 cups of water

230g of butter at
room temperature,
cubed

1 ½ cups of sugar

1 cup golden syrup

1 egg

3 cups of flour

⅓ cup milk, warmed

1 teaspoon of baking
powder

½ tablespoon of
baking soda

2 clean, empty large
tomato tins

muslin cloth

410g condensed milk

½ cup brown sugar

1 teaspoon butter

cream or ice cream

Add 2 cups of water to a camp oven and bring it to the boil to create a steam oven.

Meanwhile, cream the butter with the sugar, then mix in the golden syrup and egg. Add 2 cups of flour and mix it in.

Add both the baking powder and soda to the milk, which will froth. Mix in the remaining flour and pour it into the batter.

Line the tomato tins with buttered baking paper and pour the batter into each until they're about three-quarters full. Cover them with lightly greased muslin (or foil) and tie them closed around the edge with twine.

Place each in the boiling water, adding more if it doesn't come three-quarters up the sides of the tins. Cover with the lid and let it slowly steam for 2 to 3 hours over a very slow simmer, topping up the water as needed. The longer it steams, the better.

Meanwhile, combine the condensed milk, brown sugar and butter in a saucepan and stir until it's heated through for a simple, delicious caramel sauce.

Once the pudding is fluffy, scoop it into bowls and serve with caramel sauce and cream or vanilla ice cream.

CHOC BANANAS

I can't imagine a better summer treat than a frozen chocolate banana. The kids just love helping make them and eating them, too! I usually use hundreds and thousands for the kids' ones.

4 to 6 ripe bananas

4 bamboo sticks

$\frac{1}{4}$ cup of chopped peanuts

$\frac{1}{3}$ cup of shaved coconut

$\frac{1}{3}$ cup of shaved almonds

1 $\frac{1}{2}$ cups of dark chocolate

1 tablespoon of coconut oil

Peel the bananas and poke a stick through the middle of each, then freeze them.

Set out the peanuts, coconut and almonds on a tray, so you can dip the bananas in them later.

Boil a saucepan of water and reduce it to a low simmer once it's bubbling. Add the chocolate and coconut oil to a mixing bowl and set it over water, stirring until it melts.

Dip each banana into the chocolate and then into the nuts or coconut. Return to the freezer for 20 minutes for the chocolate to harden.

You can skip the initial freeze, instead freezing everything for 2 to 3 hours at the end, but I find the chocolate sticks better if the bananas are frozen first.

ROTISSERIE PINEAPPLE

SERVES: 4

COOK: 40-60 MIN

PREP: 5 MIN

This is the perfect after-dinner treat if you've cooked up picanha, but it's pretty special whenever you've got a campfire and a pineapple. We usually put this on as soon as the last of the picanha is off the spit. I like to take my first slices and then recoat with the sugar and cinnamon mix and put it back on to golden up.

1 large, fresh pineapple

2 tablespoons of cinnamon

2 tablespoons of brown sugar

Peel a whole fresh pineapple and thread it onto a rotisserie skewer.

In a bowl, mix cinnamon and brown sugar, then coat the pineapple generously.

Over coals at a height you can only hold your hand for 5 seconds, set it on your spit and spin it for about 40 to 60 minutes until the sugar has caramelised and the pineapple is golden brown.

ROAD TRIP BARS

We whip these up before most long road trips. They're really simple, and the kids love helping make and eat them. I bake them to give the caramel some crunch, but you can just set them in the fridge if you don't have an oven. If you don't have a blender, chop everything really finely with a knife.

1 cup of rolled oats

8 fresh medjool dates

100g of almonds

100g of hazelnuts

100g of raw cashews

100g of chia seeds

100g of dried cranberries

50g of sesame seeds

¼ cup of maple syrup

⅓ cup warm water

2 teaspoon flaky sea salt

½ cup of dark chocolate nibs

1 tablespoon of coconut oil

Blitz the oats, nuts, seeds, cranberries and 4 dates in a blender, then mix in the syrup. Press the mixture evenly into a lined baking tray, then pop it in the fridge for 10 minutes.

Blend the other 4 dates, water and half the salt to a caramel consistency. Pour it on top and bake for 10 to 18 minutes at 180°C (350°F).

Melt coconut oil with chocolate nibs in a metal or glass bowl over a pot of simmering water. Pour the chocolate over the caramel and sprinkle with flaky sea salt before placing it in the fridge to set for 30 to 40 minutes.

Enjoy with a cuppa.

SKILLET BROWNIE

Everyone loves brownie, but most of us don't have an oven to cook in when we're on the road. No worries, it's super easy in a skillet, or even a camp oven, as long as you've got a lid that fits on top and can handle some coals.

1 cup of plain flour

¾ cup of dark chocolate cocoa

¾ cup of brown sugar

1 ⅓ cup of caster sugar

175g of unsalted butter, plus extra for greasing

⅓ teaspoon of salt

1 teaspoon of vanilla extract

3 eggs

150g of dark chocolate nibs

Prepare a bed of coals away from your main fire and place a grate above it so you can cook in a skillet or camp oven over medium heat – *hot enough that you can only hold your hand 10cm above the cooking surface for 6 to 8 seconds.*

Mix the flour and cocoa in a bowl, then add brown and caster sugars, melted butter, salt, vanilla and eggs. Combine until you have a smooth consistency. Fold in the chocolate nibs.

Cut baking paper large enough to overhang your skillet (this will help when we remove the brownie), then butter the paper. Pour the batter over the baking paper and cover with a camp oven lid.

Add a light layer of coals to the lid and bake it for around 25 to 30 minutes. A good indication of when the brownie is ready is when the sides come away from the skillet.

Remove it from the skillet or camp oven carefully, lifting the baking paper. Divide it amongst your campers and enjoy it with ice cream.

TIRAMISU CUPS

SERVES: 6

PREP: 20 MIN

If we camp in one spot for a few days, this easy delight is first on the menu. It makes us dream of nights in Sardinia, Italy, with sea spray in the air and espressos on hand, with little pots of tiramisu from the corner stores.

6 egg yolks

¼ cup of castor sugar

500g of mascarpone

¼ cup of coffee liquor

1 cup of espresso

a pack of sponge
   ladyfingers
   (Savoiardi)

cocoa, for dusting

freeze-dried
   raspberries, for
   garnish

dark chocolate
   fingers, for garnish

In a mixing bowl, whisk together the egg yolks and sugar until they are well combined and become a pale yellow ribbon, similar in colour to my Kombi.

Pour in the mascarpone and continue to whisk until smooth, then drip in half the coffee liquor and mix thoroughly.

Break the half the ladyfingers to fit into 6 cups or jars – I like to make the bases thick with 2 ladyfingers in each. Mix the espresso with the remaining coffee liquor. Pour it evenly over the sponge, saving half. They don't need to be completely soaked.

Spoon half the mascarpone mixture over the ladyfingers, leaving enough room in the cup for another layer of sponge, coffee and mascarpone.

Top with a dusting of cocoa and crumb the freeze-dried raspberries. Serve with a finger of dark chocolate.

NIGHTTIME BANANA TEA

Did you know every part of a banana is edible? My grandmother used to make this for us as kids, with a cinnamon stick and honey an hour before bed.

3 cups of water or
  milk

2 banana peels

1 teaspoon of vanilla
  extract

1 stick of cinnamon

1 tablespoon honey

Bring the water or milk to a boil in a saucepan and add the leftover banana peels with vanilla extract, cinnamon and honey. Give a stir and remove from the heat.

Serve in mugs and enjoy before bed.

THE SPLITTIE

Sometimes there's nothing better than a nightcap. Whether you've just had a good, wholesome feed or spent quality time catching up with friends around the fire, there are those nights when a little something more is needed before you turn in. The Splittle is a shot we love to enjoy on those special nights, named for our van Izzie and the fact she's carried these bottles around Australia twice and then New Zealand, just for the occasions this drink is warranted. I like to think of this as a dessert in a shot and the perfect ending to a great night.

½ a ripe banana, mashed

30ml of banana liqueur

10ml of gingerbread syrup (I use Monin, but any will work)

30ml of cream

ground cinnamon

Mash the banana with a fork and add it to a cocktail shaker with the banana liqueur and a few ice cubes. Shake.

In each 60ml shot glass, pour 5ml of gingerbread syrup, slowly layer with half the banana mixture, then top with 15ml of cream and a generous sprinkle of cinnamon.

Shoot it straight down to enjoy all the flavours at once.

RED SANGRIA

I find Sangria to be one of the most refreshing drinks; chilled wine mixed with fresh fruit gives me all the summer vibes. This is one I love to break out on a nice warm day, to enjoy with some good friends.

a tray of ice cubes

½ a blood orange, sliced

½ a navel orange, sliced

½ an apple, sliced

1 cup of brandy

¾ cup of Cointreau

3 tablespoons of brown sugar

1 bottle of red wine

1 cup of orange juice

4 cinnamon sticks

Add ice, fruit, brandy, and Cointreau to a large jug. Dissolve in the sugar. Pour in the red wine and give it a great big stir.

Before serving, mix in the orange juice and garnish each glass with a cinnamon stick.

INDEX

INDEX

To my children Riley, Alba and Elsie, nothing makes me happier than being on this adventure with you.

My beloved Nanny and Papa, because of you I had a beautiful and fulfilling childhood, I will be forever grateful.

My sister Kara, I'll always treasure dancing in the kitchen with you.

To my mother and father-in-law, Jay and Hugh, thank you for being our biggest supporters and constantly letting me light fires and dig holes on your farm for a hangi. You mean the world to our family and we all adore you both.

To George and Alyce, two of the kindest and most generous souls I know. Without you, this journey wouldn't be what it is.

To Brendan and Liss, thank you for putting your trust in me and your endless support and wisdom.

Thank you to Sharnee and Art for your beautiful friendship and the prettiest picnic rugs to wander with.

To Loz and Alex, thank you for your support and constantly inspiring us. We are so grateful to you for always making sure we have hats for the road.

Thank you to our community. We have met so many wonderful people along this journey and have made lifelong friends.

The Slow Road Cookbook was first published in October 2023 by Exploring Eden Media.

ISBN: 978-0-6458988-1-1

All enquiries should be made to:
Exploring Eden Media Pty Ltd
250 Princes Highway, Bulli, NSW, 2516
publications@exploringedenmedia.com

A catalogue record for this book is available from the National Library of Australia

Author: Kirianna Poole (@theslowroad_)
Photography: Lachlan Poole
Publisher: Melissa Connell
Editor: Brendan Batty
Designer: Holly McCauley

Printed in China by Imago Group

Disclaimer: Some of the activities mentioned in this book are dangerous (and delicious). Consider your own safety and that of your companions when participating in activities referenced within, which you undertake at your own risk.

One book, one tree. This book's carbon footprint is approximately 2.5kg (5lb). But when you bought it, we planted a tree on your behalf as part of our commitment to make sure our books plant forests. Find out more about how we're making sure our books do more good than harm at **exploringedenbooks.com**.

OUR BOOKS
PLANT FORESTS

The paper used in this book was sourced from sustainable forests certified by Forest Stewardship Council® as part of our commitment to environmental responsibility. Find out more at fsc.org.

MIX
Paper | Supporting
responsible forestry
FSC® C005748

When you bought this
book, one tree was
planted